England) Johnson Club (London, George Whale, John Sargeaunt

Johnson Club Papers by various Hands

England) Johnson Club (London, George Whale, John Sargeaunt

Johnson Club Papers by various Hands

ISBN/EAN: 9783743306899

Manufactured in Europe, USA, Canada, Australia, Japa

Cover: Foto ©ninafisch / pixelio.de

Manufactured and distributed by brebook publishing software (www.brebook.com)

England) Johnson Club (London, George Whale, John Sargeaunt

Johnson Club Papers by various Hands

PREFACE

THIS Club was formed on the 13th day of December, 1884, at the "Cock Tavern," Fleet Street, London. The day was exactly one hundred years from Dr. Johnson's death, and the place was often visited by him.

Since 1884 the Club has met four times yearly, at first mostly at the "Cock," and since the old tavern was pulled down usually at the "Cheshire Cheese," but sometimes elsewhere, either near Fleet Street or at Oxford, where the Club has twice enjoyed the hospitality of Pembroke, Johnson's College; at Lichfield, his birthplace; at Cambridge, or elsewhere. At these quarterly suppers papers have been read by members; and here are some of these papers.

They are, of course, published at the "earnest

PREFACE

request of friends." Each writer is responsible only for his own contribution, and the Club is responsible for none. It still continues to drink to the pious memory of Dr. Johnson. It would wish to keep that memory green ; and it does not forget its obligations to artists, to poets, to editors, and other men, who, in different ways, have rendered this volume possible.

The following papers are published by the kind permission of the proprietors of the periodicals in which they appeared : "Boswell's Proof-sheets," from the *Atlantic Monthly;* "Dr. Johnson and the 'Gentleman's Magazine,'" from the *English Illustrated Magazine;* "Some Johnson Characteristics" and "Round the Town with Dr. Johnson," from the *Gentleman's Magazine;* and "Dr. Johnson's Politics," from the *Bookman* (New York).

G. W.
J. S.

LONDON, *June*, 1899.

TO THE EDITORS
OF THE JOHNSON CLUB MSS.

To Goldsmith's feast each diner was invited
    To bring himself and his engaging qualities.
'Twas known that if but two such guests united
    In solid talk or humorous frivolities
They entertained themselves and were delighted.
    Our club bids us, besides our personalities,
To bring sometimes to Cestrian Cheese[1] or Mitre
A block from Boswell fashioned by the writer.

I say "from Boswell," for his Life remains
    (As annotated by our Birkbeck Hill),
The great Johnsonian mine, though poorer veins,
    Yield scanty gold to labourers of skill.
But, what or whence the metal he obtains,
    The craftsman, having shaped it to his will,
Displays his product to the Brethren, who
Pronounce their judgment without more ado.

[1] "Famed Cestrian Cheese" : Phillips' "Splendid Shilling."

For some denounce the writer, some defend;
   And some bowl straight, and some deliver wides
(Excuse the metaphors, a dubious blend)
   One rhetoric, one raillery, provides;
And while some criticise and some commend,
   Each Brother says his say, and all take sides,
Save one, who through the intellectual scrimmage
Sits still and silent as a graven image.

So papers post-cœnatically read,
   Churchwarden clays and bowls of punch combined
To one high purpose, which, as Johnson said,
   Is Fellowship and free Exchange of Mind.
The warm and nimble humours long have fled,
   And left but clammy manuscripts behind.
But print the copy. Some old heart may glow,
Recalling merry nights of long ago.

                                        G. H. R.

CONTENTS

	PAGE
Verses addressed to the Editors. *George H. Radford*	vii
The Transmission of Dr. Johnson's Personality. *Augustine Birrell, Q.C., M.P.*	3
Dr. Johnson as a Grecian. *J. Gennadius*	19
Boswell's Proof-sheets. *G. B. Hill, D.C.L.*	51
The Boswell Centenary. *G. B. Hill, D.C.L.*	83
Dr. Johnson and the "Gentleman's Magazine." *A. W. Hutton*	95
Dr. Johnson's Library. *A. W. Hutton*	117
Some Johnson Characteristics. *H. W. Massingham*	133
Dr. Johnson and Lichfield. *George H. Radford*	155
Dr. Johnson and Music. *J. Sargeaunt*	173
Dr. Johnson's Politics. *J. Sargeaunt*	193
Dr. Johnson's Associations with the Law. *A. H. Spokes*	203
Dr. Johnson as a Correspondent. *A. West*	219
Round the Town with Dr. Johnson. *George Whale*	239
Dr. Johnson as a Traveller. *George Whale*	259
At the "Cheshire Cheese." *Lionel Johnson*	273

LIST OF ILLUSTRATIONS

DR. JOHNSON, AFTER SIR JOSHUA REYNOLDS. (*Photogravure*) ... ... *Frontispiece*

"Sir, among the anfractuosities of the human mind, I know not if it may not be one that there is a superstitious reluctance to sit for a picture."

THE JOHNSON CLUB ... ... *Facing page* 1
(*Drawn by F. Carruthers Gould.*)

The three portraits below are those of the early Priors: T. Fisher Unwin, the originator of the Club, the late F. W. Chesson, and E. J. Leveson. The portrait above is that of S. Rowe Bennett, the Club's first scribe.

THE COCK TAVERN (INTERIOR) *Facing page* 3

Here the Club was founded in 1884. The fittings of the room have been removed to the new tavern over the way.

LIST OF ILLUSTRATIONS

FACSIMILE OF A LETTER OF BOSWELL'S
         Facing page 19
"An odd thought strikes me: we shall receive no letters in the grave."

JAMES BOSWELL, AFTER SIR JOSHUA REYNOLDS
         Facing page 51
This kit-kat, now in the National Portrait Gallery, was painted in 1785 in accordance with a bargain proposed by Boswell, who undertook to pay for it with the first fees he received at the English Bar. He was called in Hilary term, 1786, but his "habits of conviviality" did not commend him to the creators of practice.

JAMES BOSWELL, AFTER SIR THOMAS LAWRENCE ... ...*Facing page* 83
The original is a pencil sketch. Lawrence had just entered his twenty-seventh year when Boswell died. The portrait shows the biographer in his premature decay, the victim of good nature and the grape.

ST. JOHN'S GATE, CLERKENWELL. *Facing page* 99
(*Drawn by S. J. Hodson, Brother of the Johnson Club.*)
Here was printed the *Gentleman's Magazine*. "Sir, when I first saw St. John's Gate, I beheld it with reverence."

JOHNSON IN HIS TRAVELLING DRESS *Facing page* 117
The dress may be genuine but the head clearly belongs to a different original. "He

LIST OF ILLUSTRATIONS

did not love clean linen and I have no passion for it."

TEA ... ...*Facing page* 133

This caricature was engraved by Rowlandson after a design by Samuel Collings. "My wife had tea ready for him, which it is well known he delighted to drink at all hours, particularly when sitting up late. . . . He showed much complacency upon finding that the mistress of the house was so attentive to his singular habit."

JOHNSON'S BIRTHPLACE ... ...*Facing page* 155

Michael Johnson, the Doctor's father, was born in 1656 and was a bookseller at Lichfield before 1681, when country booksellers were rare birds. In this house above the shop his son was born Sept. 18, 1709. "Salve, magna parens."

JOHNSON'S PEW IN ST. CLEMENT DANE'S CHURCH ... ...*Facing page* 173

In this church, built by Wren, Johnson worshipped for many years. Hither on Good Friday, 1773, he "carried" Boswell with him. His behaviour, as Boswell had imagined to himself, was "solemnly devout," and his diary records that he "found the service not burdensome nor tedious." Here, on April 21, 1784, Johnson, after four months'

LIST OF ILLUSTRATIONS

illness, returned thanks to God for his recovery.

INSCRIPTION ON THE PEW IN ST. CLEMENT
DANE'S ... ...*On page* 190

THE COCK TAVERN (DOORWAY) *Facing page* 193
This ancient tavern on the north side of Fleet Street has been demolished to make room for the Fleet Street branch of the Bank of England.

JOHNSON'S LODGINGS IN THE TEMPLE *Facing page* 203
In 1760 Johnson left Gray's Inn for the Temple, where he lived somewhat more than a year. "A bookish man should always have lawyers to converse with."

THE "CHESHIRE CHEESE" ...*Facing page* 219
Here the Club usually meets, the Prior sitting under the portrait of the sage. "A tavern chair is the throne of human felicity."

JOHNSON'S HOUSE IN GOUGH SQUARE *Facing page* 239
(*Drawn by Herbert Railton.*)
In this house, which still stands, Johnson lived from his fortieth to his fiftieth year, 1749–1759. Here he wrote the latter and larger part of the Dictionary, all his essays in the *Rambler*, and some numbers of the *Idler*. Here he was living when he was arrested for a debt of £5 13s. 0d. Here, in 1752, his wife died, and next day he wrote hence to

LIST OF ILLUSTRATIONS

Dr. Taylor, "Remember me in your prayers, for vain is the help of man." Here, lastly, in 1759, he wrote "Rasselas" "in the evenings of one week," for he had lost his mother and had not wherewith to pay for her funeral.

In Gough Square his garret, usually furnished with "five or six Greek folios, a deal writing-desk, and a chair and a half," was for the purposes of the Dictionary, "fitted up like a counting-house, in which he gave to the copyists their several tasks."

PLAQUE ON JOHNSON'S HOUSE IN GOUGH SQUARE
On page 256

Hardly does the stranger find Gough Square and the plaque will not tell him when Johnson lived there. His residence was from 1749 to 1759.

IONA ... ...*Facing page* 259
(*Drawn by Joseph Pennell, Brother of the Johnson Club.*)

"That illustrious island which was once the luminary of the Caledonian regions, whence savage clans and roving barbarians derived the benefits of knowledge and the blessings of religion."

THE EMBLEMS OF THE CLUB ...*Facing page* 273
(*Drawn by Joseph Pennell, Brother of the Johnson Club.*)

"I look upon it that he who does not mind his belly will hardly mind anything else."

PRIORS OF THE JOHNSON CLUB.

T. Fisher Unwin, 1885.

F. W. Chesson, 1886.

E. J. Leveson, 1887.

J. O'Connor Power, 1888.

J. Henwood Thomas, 1889.

F. Carruthers Gould, 1890.

G. Birkbeck Hill, D.C.L., 1891 and 1892.

George Whale, 1893.

G. H. Radford, 1894.

Augustine Birrell Q.C., M.P., 1895.

John Sargeaunt, 1896.

L. F. Austin, 1897.

J. Gennadius, 1898 and 1899.

Drawn by F. Carruthers Gould, Brother of the Johnson Club.

To face page 1.

THE TRANSMISSION OF
DR. JOHNSON'S PERSONALITY

A Paper read before the Johnson Club

BY

AUGUSTINE BIRRELL, Q.C., M.P.

THE COCK TAVERN, INTERIOR.
(See note in List of Illustrations.)

[To face p.]

The Transmission of Dr. Johnson's Personality

To talk about Dr. Johnson has become a confirmed habit of the British race. Four years after Johnson's death, Boswell, writing to Bishop Percy, said, "I dined at Mr. Malone's on Wednesday with Mr. W. G. Hamilton, Mr. Flood, Mr. Windham, and Mr. Courtenay, and Mr. Hamilton observed very well what a proof it was of Johnson's merit that we had been talking of him all the afternoon." That was a hundred and ten years ago. We have been talking of him ever since. But what does this perpetual interest in Dr. Johnson prove? Why, nothing whatever, except that he was interesting. But this is a great deal; indeed, it is the whole matter for a man, a woman, or a book. When you come to think of it, it is our sole demand. Just now authors, an interesting class, are displaying a great deal of uneasiness about their goods: whether they are to be in one volume or in three, how the profits (if any) are to be divided, what their books should be about, and how far the laws of decency should be observed in their construction. All this is very wearisome to the reader, who does not care whether a book be as long as "Clarissa Harlowe," or as short as "The Luck of Roaring Camp," provided only and always that it is interesting. And this is why Johnson is supreme, and why we go on talking about him long after we have exhausted the subject of our next-door neighbour.

Not many years ago, at our own annual gathering on the 13th of December, two of our guests were called upon (the practice is inhospitable) to say something. One was an Irish patriot, who had languished in jail during a now ancient *régime*, who on demanding from the chaplain to be provided with some book which was not the Bible, a collection of writings with which he was already, so he assured the chaplain, well acquainted, was supplied with Boswell, a book, it so chanced, he had never before read. He straightway, so he told us, forgot both his own and his country's woes. "How happily the days of Thalaba went by," and now, in the retrospect of life, his prison days wear the hues of enjoyment and delight. He has since ceased to be a patriot, but he remains a Boswellian.

The other guest was no less or more than the gigantic Bonnor, the Australian cricketer. He told us that until that evening he had never heard of Dr. Johnson. Thereupon somebody, I hope it was the

DR. JOHNSON'S PERSONALITY

patriot, and not a member of the club, was thoughtless enough to titter audibly. "Yes," added Bonnor, in heightened tones, and drawing himself proudly up, "and what is more, I come from a great country, where you might ride a horse sixty miles a day for three months, and never meet anybody who had. But," so he proceeded, "I have heard of him now, and can only say that were I not Bonnor the cricketer, I would be Samuel Johnson." He sat down amidst applause, and the sorrowful conviction straightway seized hold of me that could the Doctor have obtained permission to revisit Fleet Street, his earthly heaven, that night, and had he come in amongst us, he would certainly have preferred both the compliment and the conversation of the cricketer to those of the critics he would have found at the table.

This, at all events, is what I mean by being interesting.

But how does it come about that we can all at this distance of time be so infatuated about a man who was not a great philosopher or poet, but only a miscellaneous writer? The answer must be, Johnson's is a transmitted personality.

To transmit personality is the secret of literature, as surely as the transmission of force is the mainspring of the universe. It is also the secret of religion.

To ask how it is done is to break your heart. Genius can do it sometimes, but what cannot genius do? Talent fails oftener than it succeeds. Mere sincerity of purpose is no good at all, unless accompanied by the rare gift of personal expression. A rascal like Benvenuto Cellini, or Casanova, an oddity like Borrow, is more likely to possess this gift than a saint; and this is why it is so much to be regretted that we have fewer biographies of avowed rogues than of professed saints. But I will not pursue this branch of the subject further.

Johnson's, I repeat, is a transmitted personality. We know more about him than we do about anybody else in the wide world. Chronologically speaking, he might have been one of the four great grandfathers of most of us. But what do any of you know about that *partie carré* of your ancestors. What were their habits and customs? Did they wear tye-wigs or bob-wigs? What were their opinions? Can you tell me a single joke they ever made? Who were their intimate friends? What was their favourite dish? They lived and died. The truth is, we inhabit a world which has been emptied of our predecessors. Perhaps it is as well; it leaves the more room for us to occupy the stage during the short time we remain upon it.

But though we cannot acquire the secret; though we cannot deliberately learn how to transmit personality from one century to another, either our own personality or anybody else's, still, we may track the path and ask by what ways may personality be transmitted.

Dr. Johnson's case is in the main that of a person-

DR. JOHNSON'S PERSONALITY

ality transmitted to us by means of a great biography. He comes down to us through Boswell. To praise Boswell is superfluous. His method was natural and therefore, I need not add, intensely original. He had always floating through his fuddled brain a great ideal of portraiture. Johnson himself, though he does not seem to have had any confidence in his disciple, preferring to appoint the unclubable Hawkins his literary executor, nevertheless furnished Boswell with hints and valuable directions; but the credit is all Boswell's, whose one aim was to make his man live. To do this he was prepared, like a true artist, to sacrifice everything. The proprieties did not exist for him. Then, what a free hand he had. Johnson left neither wife nor child. I don't suppose Black Frank, Johnson's servant and residuary legatee, ever read a line of the "Biography." There was no daughter married to a country squire to put her pen through the fact that Johnson's father kept a bookstall. There was no grandson in the Church to water down the witticisms that have reverberated through the world. He was tendered plenty of bad advice. He coarsely rejected it. Miss Hannah More besought his tenderness "for our virtuous and most revered departed friend, I beg you will mitigate some of his asperities." To which Boswell replied that he would not cut off his claws nor make a tiger a cat to please anybody.

The excellent Bishop Percy humbly requested Boswell that his (the Bishop's) name might be suppressed in the pages of the forthcoming "Biography." To him Boswell—"As to suppressing your lordship's name, I will do anything to oblige your lordship but that very thing. I owe to the authenticity of my work to introduce as many names of eminent persons as I can. Believe me, my lord, you are not the only Bishop in the number of great men with which my pages are graced. *I am resolute as to this matter.*"

This sets me thinking of the many delightful pages of the great "Biography" in which the name of Percy occurs, in circumstances to which one can understand the Bishop objecting. So absurd a creature is man, particularly what Carlyle used to call shovel-hatted man.

How easily might the greatest of our biographies have been whittled away to nothing—to the dull ineptitudes with which we are all familiar, but for the glorious intrepidity of Boswell, who, if he did not practise the whole duty of man, at least performed the whole duty of a biographer.

As a means of transmitting personality memoirs rank high. Here we have Miss Burney's "Memoirs" to help us, and richly do they repay study, and Mrs. Thrale's marvellous collection of anecdotes, sparkling with womanly malice. Less deserving of notice are the volumes of Miss Anna Seward's correspondence, edited by Sir Walter Scott, who did not choose for their motto, as he fairly might have done, Sir Toby Belch's famous observation to that superlative fool Sir

DR. JOHNSON'S PERSONALITY

Andrew Aguecheek, " Let there be gall enough in thy ink though thou write with a goose-pen—no matter."

But whether we read the " Biography " or the " Memoirs," it cannot escape our notice that Johnson's personality has been transmitted to us chiefly by a record of his *talk*.

It is a perilous foundation on which to build reputation, for it rests upon the frail testimony of human memory and human accuracy. How comes it that we are all well persuaded that Boswell and the rest of the recorders did not invent Johnson's talk, but that it has come down to us bearing his veritable image and superscription? It is sometimes lightly said that had we records of other men's talk it would be as good as Johnson's. It is Boswells who are the real want. This I deny.

To be a great table-talker—and be it borne in mind a good deal of what is sometimes called table-talk is not table-talk at all, but extracts from common-place books and carefully doctored notes—you must have *first* a *marked* and *constant* character, and, *second*, the gift of characteristic expression, so as to stamp all your utterances, however varied, however flatly contradictory one with another, with certain recognisable and ever-present marks or notes. The great Duke of Wellington possessed these qualifications, and consequently, though his conversation, as recorded by Lord Stanhope and others, is painfully restricted in its range of subject, and his character is lacking in charm, it is always interesting and sometimes remarkable. All the stories about Wellington are characteristic, and so are all the stories about Johnson. They all fit in with our conception of the character of the man about whom they are told, and thus strengthen and confirm that unity of impression which is essential if personality is to be transmitted down the ages.

The last story of Johnson I stumbled across is in a little book called "A Book for a Rainy Day," written by an old gentleman called Smith, the author of a well-known life of Nollekens, the sculptor, a biography written with a vein of causticity some have attributed to the fact that the biographer was not also a legatee. Boswell, thank Heaven, was above such considerations. He was not so much as mentioned in his great friend's will. The hated Hawkins was preferred to him; Hawkins, who wrote the authorised "Life of Johnson," in which Boswell's name is only mentioned once, in a foot-note. But to return to Mr. Smith. In this book of his he records : "I once saw Johnson follow a sturdy thief who had stolen his handkerchief in Grosvenor Square, seize him by the collar with both hands, and shake him violently, after which he quickly let him loose, and then with his open hand gave him so powerful a smack on the face as to send him off the pavement staggering."

Now, in this anecdote of undoubted authenticity Johnson said nothing whatever, he fired off no epigram, thundered no abuse, and yet the story is as charac-

DR. JOHNSON'S PERSONALITY

teristic as his famous encounter with the Thames bargee.

You must have the character first and the talk comes afterwards. It is the old story; anybody can write like Shakespeare, if he has the mind.

But still, for this talk Johnson possessed great qualities. Vast and varied was his information on all kinds of subjects. He knew not only books, but a great deal about trades and manufactures, ways of existence, customs of business. He had been in all sorts of societies; kept every kind of company. He had fought the battle of life in a hand-to-hand encounter; had slept in garrets; had done hack work for booksellers; in short, had lived on fourpence halfpenny a day. By the side of Johnson, Burke's knowledge of men and things was bookish and notional. He had a great range of fact. Next, he had a strong mind operating upon and in love with life. He never lost his curiosity in his fellow-men.

Then he had, when stirred by contact with his friends, or inflamed by the desire of contradiction, an amazingly ready wit and a magnificent vocabulary always ready for active service in the field. Add to this, extraordinary, and at times an almost divine tenderness, a deep-rooted affectionateness of disposition, united to a positively brutal aversion to any kind of exaggeration, particularly of feelings, and you get a combination rarely to be met with.

Another point must not be forgotten—ample

leisure. The Dr. Johnson we know is the *post-pension* Doctor. Never, surely, before or since did three hundred pounds a year of public money yield (thanks mainly to Boswell) such a perpetual harvest for the public good. Not only did it keep the Doctor himself and provide a home for Mrs. Williams and Mrs. Desmoulins and Miss Carmichael and Mr. Levett, but it has kept us all going ever since. Dr. Johnson after his pension, which he characteristically wished was twice as large, so that the newspaper dogs might make twice as much noise about it, was a thoroughly lazy fellow, who hated solitude with the terrible hatred of inherited melancholia. He loved to talk, and he hated to be alone. He said, " John Wesley's conversation is good, but he is never at leisure. He is always obliged to go at a certain hour. This is very disagreeable to a man who loves to fold his legs and have out his talk, as I do."

But of course Wesley—a bright and glorious figure of the last century, to whom justice will some day be done when he gets from under the huge human organisation which has so long lain heavily on the top of him—Wesley had on his eager mind and tender conscience the conversion of England, whose dark places he knew; he could not stop all night exchanging intellectual hardihood with Johnson. Burke, too, had his plaguey politics, to keep Lord John Cavendish up to the proper pitch of an uncongenial enthusiasm, and all sorts of entanglements and even lawsuits of his

DR. JOHNSON'S PERSONALITY

own; Thurlow had the woolsack; Reynolds, his endless canvasses and lady sitters; Gibbon, his history; Beauclerk, his assignations. One by one these eminent men would get up and steal away, but Johnson remained behind.

To sum this up, I say, it is to his character, *plus* his mental endowments, as exhibited by his talk, as recorded by Boswell and others, that the great world of Englishmen owe their Johnson. Such sayings as "Hervey was a vicious man, but he was very kind to me; if you call a dog Hervey I should love him," throb through the centuries and excite in the mind a devotion akin to, but different from, religious feeling. The difference is occasioned by the entire absence of the note of sanctity. Johnson was a good man and a pious man, and a great observer of days; but despite his bow to an archbishop, he never was in the way of becoming a saint. He lived fearfully, prayerfully, but without assurance or exaltation.

Another mode of the transmission of personality is by letters. To be able to say what you mean in a letter is a useful accomplishment, but to say what you mean in such a way as at the same time to say what you are is immortality. To publish a man's letters after his death is nowadays a familiar outrage; they often make interesting volumes, seldom permanent additions to our literature. Lord Beaconsfield's letters to his sister are better than most, but of the letter writers of our own day Mrs. Carlyle stands proudly first—her stupendous lord being perhaps a good second.

Johnson's letters deserve more praise than they have received. To win that praise they only require a little more attention. Dr. Birkbeck Hill has collected them in two stately volumes, and they form an excellent appendix to his great edition of the Life. They are in every style, from the monumental to the utterly frivolous, but they are always delightful and ever characteristic. Their friendliness—an excellent quality in a letter—is perhaps their most prominent feature. It is hardly ever absent. Next to their friendliness comes their playfulness; gaiety, indeed, their is none. At heart our beloved Doctor was full of gloom, but though he was never gay, he was frequently playful, and his letters abound with an innocent and touching mirth and an always affectionate fun. Some of his letters, those, for example, to Miss Porter after his mother's death, are, I verily believe, as moving as any ever written by man. They reveal, too, a thoughtfulness and a noble generosity it would be impossible to surpass. I beseech you to read Dr. Johnson's letters; they are full of literature, and with what is better than literature, life and character and comradeship. Had we nothing of Johnson but his letters, we should know him and love him.

Of his friend Sir Joshua's two most famous pictures I need not speak. One of them is the best known portrait in our English world. It has more than a trace of the vile melancholy the sitter inherited from his father, a melancholy which I fear turned some hours of every one of his days into blank dismay and wretchedness.

At last, by a route not I hope wearisomely circuitous, we reach Johnson's own books, his miscellaneous writings, his twelve volumes octavo, and the famous Dictionary.

It is sometimes lightly said, "Oh, nobody reads Johnson," just as it is said, "Nobody reads Richardson, nobody reads Sterne, nobody reads Byron"! It is all nonsense; there is always somebody reading Johnson, there is always somebody weeping over Richardson, there is always somebody sniggering over Sterne and chuckling over Byron. It is no disrespect to subsequent writers of prose or poetry to say that none of their productions do or ever can supply the place of the "Lives of the Poets," of "Clarissa," of the Elder Shandy and his brother Toby, or of "Don Juan." Genius is never crowded out.

But I am willing enough to admit that Johnson was more than a writer of prose, more than a biographer of poets; he was himself a poet, and his poetry, as much as his prose, nay, more than his prose, because of its concentration, conveys to us the same dominating personality that bursts from the pages of Boswell like the genii from the bottle in the Arabian story.

Of poetic freedom he had barely any. He knew but one way of writing poetry, namely, to chain together as much sound sense and sombre feeling as he could squeeze into the fetters of rhyming couplets, and then to clash those fetters loudly in your ear. This proceeding he called versification. It is simple, it is monotonous, but in the hands of Johnson it sometimes does not fall far short of the moral sublime. "London" and the "Vanity of Human Wishes" have never failed to excite the almost passionate admiration of succeeding poets. Ballantyne tells us how Scott avowed he had more pleasure in reading "London" and the "Vanity of Human Wishes" than any other poetical compositions he could mention, and adds, "I think I never saw his countenance more indicative of high admiration than while reciting them aloud."

Byron loved them; they never failed to move Tennyson to cries of approval. There is, indeed, that about them which stamps them great. They contain lines which he could easily have bettered, verbosities a child can point out; but the effect they produce, on learned and simple, on old and young, is one and the same. We still hear the voice of Johnson, as surely as if he had declaimed the verses into a phonograph.

When you turn to them you are surprised to find how well you know them, what a hold they have got upon the English mind, how full of quotations they are, how immovably fixed in the glorious structure of English verse. Poor Sprat has perished despite his splendid tomb in the Abbey. Johnson has only a cracked stone and a worn-out inscription (for the Hercules in St. Paul's is unrecognisable), but he dwells where he would wish to dwell—in the loving memory of men.

DR JOHNSON AS A GRECIAN

A Paper read before the Johnson Club
BY
J. GENNADIUS
On June 28, 1898

Dear Sir

When Mr Johnson and I arrived at Inverary after our expedition to the Hebrides, and there for the first time after many days renewed our enjoyment of the luxuries of civilized life, one of the most elegant that I could wish to find, was lying for me — a letter from Mr Garrick.

I hope Mr Johnson has given you an entertaining account of his northern Tour. He is certainly to favour the world with some of his Remarks.

James Boswell

Edinburgh
11 April 1774.

Dr. Johnson as a Grecian

I HAVE always felt that I was hardly competent to produce a paper such as would merit your attention or respond to your expectations. And this is my excuse for deferring so long what I deem a privilege as well as an obligation. However, I have written a paper of a sort; and its perusal will, I am afraid, convince you that my misgivings were not without reason.

I have at least endeavoured to choose a safe, not to say familiar, ground; and on going over it I was rejoiced to find that, so far as I am aware, no one has availed himself of a theme which occupies a large and important place in the life-work of the Master. This abstention on the part of those who have preceded me I can only account for as an act of thoughtful courtesy, if I may say so, towards me; for it is my purpose to speak to you of Dr. Johnson as a Grecian.

And I shall begin by asking you to consider how entirely Socratic in its method was his lifelong teaching; I will remind you that it was in this very neighbourhood of Hampstead that he proved himself superior even to his prototype in marital virtues, in his blind devotion to a motherly wife. For, whereas Socrates left his sweet-tempered Xanthippe slaving away at home, while he trifled in the Agora, Mrs. Johnson, we are told, "indulged herself in country air and nice living at an unsuitable expense (at Hampstead), while her husband was drudging in the smoke of London; and that she by no means treated him with that complacency which is the most engaging quality of a wife. But all this is perfectly compatible with his fondness for her, especially when it is remembered that he had a high opinion of her understanding, and that the impressions which her beauty, real or imaginary, had originally made upon his fancy, being continued by habit, had not been effaced, though she herself was doubtless much altered for the worse."

No wonder it was, during the rare whiffs of fresh air which the gentle Mrs. Johnson allowed him, that he betook himself (at Hampstead in 1749) to the composition of "The Vanity of Human Wishes;" and when at last his effulgent and elderly siren disappeared, he kept up his lamentations in Greek. "You know," he wrote to Th. Warton, "poor Dodsley has lost his wife. I believe he is much affected; I hope he will not suffer so much as I yet suffer from the loss of mine. Οἴμοι! τί δ' οἴμοι; θνητὰ γὰρ πεπόνθαμεν." (Alas! but wherefore alas? We have suffered the woes of mortals.) The quotation was aptly chosen. It is from "Bellerophon," one of the lost plays of Euripides (apud Suidam); and

DR. JOHNSON AS A GRECIAN

Euripides was an earlier and more abiding love of his than even Mrs. Johnson.

"He told me (says Boswell) what he read *solidly* at Oxford was Greek; not the Grecian historians, but Homer and Euripides, and now and then a little Epigram." What Boswell means by this quaint expression, "a little Epigram," is, no doubt, parts of the "Anthologia,"—of which more anon. But, referring to Johnson's attempt at a methodical course of studies at Oxford, Boswell again says:—"I find a number of lines of two of Euripides' tragedies . . . and some part of Theocritus." On another occasion "armorial bearings having been mentioned, Johnson said they were as ancient as the siege of Thebes, which he proved by a passage in one of the tragedies of Euripides."[1] And on June 19, 1794, Boswell notes: "He was not well to-day and said very little, employing himself chiefly in reading Euripides."

Even before going up to Oxford he had a wider knowledge of Greek than was usual at that time. "What he read during those two years, he told me,"

---

[1] "Phœnissæ, 1120, I imagine," adds Boswell, jun. But this line—

Τυδεὺς, λέοντος δέρος ἔχων ἐπ' ἀσπίδα,

is only one of the six armorial bearings described in The Phœnissæ (1107–9, 1114–18, 1120–22, 1125, 1130–32, 1135) in imitation of the still earlier and more detailed account of Æschylus ("The Seven against Thebes," 387–648) of the devices of the chiefs, on two of whose shields mottoes are also inscribed. So that also this much prized adjunct of mediæval chivalry is of Greek origin. Among Johnson's other Latin renderings of Greek verse there is the well-known passage in Euripides' "Medea," 193–203 ("Works," Oxf. 1825, I. 191).

says Boswell, "was not works of mere amusement, 'not voyages and travels, but all literature, Sir, all ancient writers, all manly; though but little Greek; only Anacreon and Hesiod.'"[1] To Anacreon, like the ladies' man he was (in spite of Mrs. Johnson), he remained faithful to the end, as we shall see. But in the statement just quoted he rather underrates his early proficiency in Greek, if we are to judge from his very creditable translation, while at Stourbridge school, of that most beautiful of Homeric passages, the dialogue of Hector and Andromache, as well as from the "Designs," as he calls them, of the various works he projected. In this list, drawn up early in life, and added to in 1752 and 1753, the following entries refer to Greek literature alone :—

"Aristotle's Rhetorick, a translation of it into English.—Aristotle's Ethicks, an English translation of them, with notes.—Translation of the 'History of Herodian.'—Hierocles upon Pythagoras, translated into English, perhaps with notes.[2]—From Ælian, a

---

[1] This was at the age of nineteen. And he adds : "When I came to Oxford Dr. Adams, now Master of Pembroke College, told me that I was the best qualified for the University that he had ever known come there." Considering the scholarly equipment even of professors, in those days, the praise appears now but faint. Lord Chesterfield in a letter to his son (1748) urges him to consider the advantages of a Greek professorship in one of the Universities—a snug sinecure, requiring but meagre knowledge of the language. Referring to some reminiscences of Mr. Edwards, as to the respect and fear with which he inspired his fellow-students, Johnson remarked :—"Sir, they respected me for my literature; and yet it was not great, but by comparison."

[2] In a note, added later, he remarks "This is done by Norris."

volume of select stories, perhaps from others.—Plutarch's lives in English, with notes.—Coluthus, to be translated.—Classical Miscellanies ; Select translations from Ancient Greek and Latin authors.—Maximes, Characters and Sentiments, after the manner of Bruyère, collected out of ancient authors, particularly the Greek, with apophthegms.—Lives of the Philosophers,[1] written with a polite air, in such a manner as may divert as well as instruct."—There are also projects of a history of Mythology, a history of the Revival of Classic Learning in Europe, &c.

His own modest estimate of his knowledge of Greek is accounted for by the very fact that he knew what it is to know Greek thoroughly. "Mr. Beauclerk told Dr. Johnson that Dr. James said to him he knew more Greek than Mr. Walmesley. 'Sir,' said he, 'Dr. James did not know enough Greek to be sensible of his ignorance. Walmesley did.'" And, being asked if Barnes knew a good deal of Greek, he answered, "I doubt, Sir, he was *unoculus inter cæcos*."

Very much in this sense is Ford's anecdote :[2] "Here the conversation turned one morning on a Greek criticism of Dr. Johnson in some volume lying on the table, which I ventured (for I was then young) to deem incorrect, and pointed it out to him [Jacob Bryant]. I could not help thinking that he was some-

---

[1] Most probably after Diogenes Laertius, from whom he repeatedly quotes in his conversations.
[2] Gifford's "Works of Ford," I. lxii.

what of my opinion, but was cautious and reserved. 'But, Sir,' said I, willing to overcome his scruples, 'Dr. Johnson himself admitted that he was not a good Greek scholar.' 'Sir,' he replied with a serious and impressive air, 'it is not easy for us to say what such a man as Johnson would call a good Greek scholar.'"

The reason why the notion obtained currency that Johnson was not a Hellenist is best explained by Dr. Parr, who, with characteristic self-complacency, claimed to be the most eminent Greek scholar in England, next to Porson.[1] He says, "Dr. Johnson was an admirable scholar.[2] . . . The classical scholar was forgotten in the great original contributor to the literature of his country." Similar is the testimony in M. Tyers' "Biographical Sketch": "He (Johnson) owned that many knew more Greek than himself, but that his grammar would show he had once taken pains. Sir Wm. Jones, one of the most enlightened of the sons of men, as Johnson described him, has often said he knew a great deal of Greek."

[1] He said: "There are three great Grecians in England; Porson is the first, Burney is the third, and who is the second I need not say." W. Field's "Memoirs of the Rev. Samuel Parr," London, 1828, ii. p. 215.

[2] Johnson always spoke of himself as a "scholar," *i.e.*, a man of letters, possessing a mastery of both ancient and modern literature. In this sense he uses the word in "The Vanity of Human Wishes," and so he styles himself in his letters to Lord Chesterfield, and in a letter to the King's Librarian. As such, he was, perhaps, the one man best qualified to write (1763) the "Life of Ascham," his forerunner in scholarship and the love of Greek, and, in many respects, his counterpart in character.

DR. JOHNSON AS A GRECIAN

But the question is set at rest by Boswell, when he says: "A very erroneous notion has circulated as to Johnson's deficiency in the knowledge of the Greek language, partly owing to the modesty with which, knowing how much there was to be learnt, he used to mention his own comparative acquisitions. When Mr. Cumberland talked to him of the Greek fragments which are so well illustrated in *The Observer*, and of the Greek dramatists in general, he candidly acknowledged his insufficiency in that particular branch of Greek literature. Yet it may be said that, though not a great, he was a good Greek scholar. Dr. Charles Burney, the younger, who is universally acknowledged by the best judges to be one of the few men of this age who are very eminent for their skill in that noble language, has assured me that Johnson could give a Greek word for almost every English one; and that, although not sufficiently conversant in the niceties of the language, he upon some occasions discovered, even in these, a considerable degree of critical acumen. Dr. Dalzel, Professor of Greek at Edinburgh, whose skill in it is unquestionable, mentioned to me, in very liberal terms, the impression which was made upon him by Johnson, in a conversation which they had in London concerning that language. As Johnson, therefore, was undoubtedly one of the first Latin scholars in modern times, let us not deny to his fame some additional splendour from Greek."

That Johnson often displayed "a considerable degree

of critical acumen," as regards Greek, is amply shown from his remarks on Potter's translation of Æschylus. When (1778) asked by Garrick, "And what think you, sir, of it?" Johnson replied, "I thought what I read of it, *verbiage;* but upon Mr. Harris's recommendation I will read a play. (And to Harris), Don't prescribe two." On another occasion, Boswell says, "As an instance of the niceness of his taste, though he praised [Gilbert] West's translation of Pindar [London, 1749], he pointed out the following passage as faulty, by expressing a circumstance so minute as to detract from the general dignity which should prevail :—

> Down then from thy glittering *nail*,
> Take, O Muse, thy Dorian lyre."

The juxtaposition of the Greek text (Olym. I. 25)

> —ἀλλὰ Δωρίαν ἀπὸ φόρμιγγα πασσάλου
> λάμβανε,

renders the delicacy of Johnson's appreciation all the more evident.[1] Like acumen is manifest in his remark "that the delineation of character in the end of the first book of 'The Retreat of the Ten Thousand' was the first instance of the kind that was known."

[1] Johnson included West's translation in "The Works of the English Poets"; and his criticism of it shows a thorough insight into the power and beauty of the Greek text. "A work of this kind," he says in his preface, "must, in a minute examination, discover many imperfections; but West's version, so far as I have considered it, appears to be a product of great labour and great abilities."

DR. JOHNSON AS A GRECIAN

The incident related by Baretti to Malone (Prior's "Malone," p. 160) may also be quoted here: "Dr. James picked up on a stall a book of Greek hymns. He brought it to Johnson, who ran his eyes over the pages and returned it. A year or two afterwards he dined at Sir Joshua Reynolds's with Dr. Musgrave, the editor of Euripides. Musgrave made a great parade of his Greek learning, and among other less-known writers mentioned these hymns, which he thought none of the company were acquainted with, and extolled highly. Johnson said the first of them was indeed very fine, and immediately repeated it. It consisted of ten or twelve lines."[1]

It is nevertheless certain that, in his earlier struggles for existence, Johnson had neglected Greek. "He renewed his Greek some years ago," says Tyers, "for which he found no occasion for twenty years." And Croker (p. 795), although he questions the fact, on insufficient grounds as I think, yet records that "it has been said that Dr. Johnson never exerted such

---

[1] Here again the editors leave us in the dark. I think, however, there is little doubt the hymn in question is the "Thanksgiving at Lamp-lighting," Ἐπιλύχνιος Εὐχαριστία, sung at Evensong, one of the earliest Christian hymns, which, St. Basil says (De Spir. Sanct. c. 29), was already considered old at his day (390). It is composed of just 13 lines (Φῶς ἱλαρὸν ἁγίας δόξης, &c.) of surpassing beauty, such as to have captivated Johnson's attention and memory. It has been translated repeatedly: into English by G. W. Bethune and by the late Archbishop Benson. The book picked up by Dr. James must have been Ch. Pelargus's "Enchiridion Græco-Latinum hymnorum, cantionum et precationum quas christiani Græci hodie recitant. Francofurti, 1594;" in which this hymn occurs.

steady application as he did for the last ten years of his life in the study of Greek."

What appears to have rekindled his ardour for the language is the incident related by Mrs. Piozzi: "When the King of Denmark was in England (in 1768) one of his noblemen was brought by Mr. Coleman to see Dr. Johnson at Mr. Thrale's country house; and having heard, he said, that he was not famous for Greek literature, attacked him on the weak side, politely adding that he chose that conversation on purpose, to favour himself. Dr. Johnson, however, displayed so copious a knowledge of authors, books, and every branch of learning in that language, that the gentleman appeared astonished. When he was gone Johnson said: 'Now, for all this triumph I may thank Thrale's Xenophon here; as, I think, excepting that *one*, I have not looked in a Greek book these ten years. But see what haste my dear friends were all in,' continued he, 'to tell this poor innocent foreigner that I knew nothing of Greek! Oh, no! he knows nothing of Greek!' with a loud burst of laughter."

After this triumph he was evidently enamoured with Xenophon. His reference to the delineation of character in the "Anabasis" was made subsequently to this incident, and, ten years later, in introducing Dr. Burney, who desired to consult a Welsh MS. in the Bodleian, he wrote (Nov. 2, 1778) to Dr. Edwards: "But we must not let Welsh drive us from Greek. What comes of Xenophon? If you do not like the trouble of publishing the book, do not let your commentaries be lost; contrive that they may be published somewhere." Boswell's editors mention that an edition of the "Memorabilia" was then being prepared by Dr. Edwards, but do not state who he was and whether the book was ever published. It was, as a matter of fact, issued by H. Owen, with a short preface from the Clarendon Press in 1875.[1] Edward Edwards appears to have been Johnson's fellow student referred to above (p. 22) and was then a Fellow of St. John's.

"Greek, sir, is like lace; every man gets as much of it as he can." The simile is not Mrs. Johnson's, or any other lady's. It is the Doctor's own.[2] For he had a special fondness for lace, and indignantly characterised as "absurd" Sir Joshua Reynolds's remark that "nobody wore laced coats now." He himself made his appearance on the first representation of his "Irene" bedecked in a scarlet waistcoat with rich gold lace, and carrying a gold-laced hat.

The importance he attached to classic studies appears from his statement to Boswell, who having got him fast in a sculler, began to cross-question him on their way to Greenwich. "I asked him if he really

---

[1] Since writing the above I find that in a note to Johnson's letter to the Rev. William Adams (July 11, 1784), in which reference is made to Edwards's edition of the "Memorabilia," Dr. G. B. Hill ("Johnson's Letters," ii. 409) mentions the publication of that work.

[2] Most likely he had in his mind the French saying: "Quand on prend du galon on si'en saurait trop prendre."

thought a knowledge of the Greek and Latin languages an essential to a good education. Johnson: 'Most certainly, sir; for those who know them have a very great advantage over those who do not. Nay, sir, it is wonderful what a difference learning makes upon people, even in the common intercourse of life, which does not appear to be much connected with it.'"

And on another occasion, " having regretted to him that I had learnt little Greek, as is too generally the case in Scotland; that I had for a long time hardly applied at all to the study of that noble language, and that I was desirous of being told by him what method to follow; he recommended to me as easy helps, Sylvanus's 'First Book of the Iliad'; Dawson's 'Lexicon of the Greek New Testament'; and 'Hesiod' with 'Porson's Lexicon' at the end of it." And again: "He roused me with manly and spirited conversation. He advised me . . . to apply to Greek an hour every day."

Johnson himself appeared to have followed this precept; and his inmost thoughts, his most cherished yearning, he recorded in Greek. On July 25, 1776 he indited a special prayer beseeching God "to look with mercy upon his studies and endeavours"; and from a subjoined note it appears that this referred to his resolve " to apply vigorously to study, particularly of the Greek and Italian languages." His eagerness for Italian may be explained by the fact that about that time Piozzi first appeared upon the scene.

DR. JOHNSON AS A GRECIAN

On April 4, 1779, he notes in his "Prayers and Meditations": "At the Altar I commended my Θ. Φ., and again I prayed the prayer." On Easter Day, 1781, he again writes: "I commended my Θ. friends, as I have formerly done." Over the meaning of these two mysterious Greek letters a lively controversy arose. The more prosaic, and no doubt accurate, explanation advanced, is that they stand for θανόντες φίλοι, "departed friends." But a professed insight into the yearning of Dr. Johnson's tender heart has suggested that they signify "Thrale friends."[1]

At the age of 63 he made the following entry: "Easter Day (1772), after twelve at night. The day is now begun on which I hope to begin a new course, ὥς περ ἀφ' ὑσπλήγγων" (as from the starting place). The phrase is taken from the Athletics of the Greeks, and may be rendered in familiar parlance as "turning

---

[1] "Gentleman's Magazine," 1838, ii. 364. Macaulay, in his first essay on Johnson (Sept. 1831), deservedly belabours Croker for inferring that θ stands for θνητοί, and for supposing that this word, which really means *mortals*, can be rendered by *departed*.

Dr. G. Birkbeck Hill has kindly communicated to me the following, which occurs in the "Remains of Thomas Hearne" (Ed. 1869, I. 208) under date of Oct. 26, 1710:—

"When any monument in the old time was erected to the memory of several persons, they put the mark Θ to denote such persons as were dead, and the mark V for those that were living. Thus we have this instance in Lipsius: *De recta Pronuntiatione Latinæ Linguæ*, p. 75:—

      Θ N. Oogubrius. Cn. L. Nicephorus.
      Θ Gulnia. Cn. L. Nice.
      V L. Safinius. d. L. Surus.

where the two former marks signify that the persons were dead, and the latter that he was living; and there are other examples there."

over a new leaf." There appears to have been good cause for this pious resolve. On the previous day Dr. Johnson had made the following entry: "I read the Greek Testament without construing, and this day concluded the Apocalypse." It is of that very day that Boswell relates: "I paid him a short visit both on Friday and Saturday, and seeing his large folio Greek Testament before him, beheld him with a reverential awe, and would not intrude upon his time."

Now, Boswell does not confess why this discreet forbearance, so unusual in him. The fact is, his reverential awe at the sight of the large folio Greek Testament was the effect of what had happened to Thomas Osborne, the bookseller, who, having ventured to worry the Doctor when seriously occupied, was knocked down with the volume in question. For Boswell relates the occurrence: "The simple truth I had from Johnson himself, 'Sir, he was impertinent to me, and I beat him. But it was not in his shop; it was in my own chambers.'" And to Mrs. Thrale, who questioned him, Johnson said: "There is nothing to tell, dear Madam, but that he was insolent, and I beat him; and he was a blockhead and told of it, which I should never have done. . . . I have beaten many a fellow, but the rest had the wit to hold their tongues." The Doctor, you will observe, suppresses the fact that he made a militant use of the sacred volume which he was reading for his spiritual edification. But the historic folio,

DR. JOHNSON AS A GRECIAN

which, it appears, included the Septuagint, and thus added to Johnson's innate pugnacity, was to be seen in its belaboured condition at a bookseller's in Cambridge as late as 1812[1]—a warning to the like of Osborne, "a man," as Johnson said, "entirely destitute of shame, without sense of any disgrace but poverty." Osborne had even the honour of being introduced in the "Dunciad" by Pope; but, as Johnson goes on to say, "the shafts of satire . . . were deadened by his impassive dulness" ("Works," viii. 302).

Thus Johnson had recourse to Greek Scripture, as to a daily mentor, guardian, and guide. "I observed upon the dial plate of his watch," says Boswell, "a short Greek inscription taken from the New Testament, νὺξ γὰρ ἔρχεται, being the first words of our Saviour's solemn admonition to the improvement of that time which is allowed us to prepare for eternity: 'The night cometh when no man can work'" (John ix. 4).

[1] "The identical book with which Johnson knocked down Osborne (Biblia Græca Septuaginta, Fo. 1594, Frankfort; the note written by the Rev. — Mills) I saw in Feb. 1812 at Cambridge, in the possession of J. Thorpe, bookseller, whose catalogue, since published, contains particulars authenticating the assertion" (Nichol's Lit. Ann. viii. 446). In appending this note to Mrs. Thrale's narrative of the occurrence Dr. G. B. Hill ("Johnson's Miscellanies," i. 304) adds: "This Fo. is not mentioned in the sale catalogue of Johnson's library. It is scarcely likely that Osborne brought it to Johnson's chambers as schoolboys used to provide the birch-rods with which they were beaten." I confess I fail to seize the point. Surely all the books Johnson ever possessed were not included in the catalogue of the sale of his library. Moreover Nichol's statement is circumstantial.

In like manner, Johnson's usual seal was a head of Homer. (But Dr. Johnson and Homer may well serve as the special subject of some future paper—provided always you do not succumb under the infliction of the present one.) Writing to Langton (July 5, 1774) he says, "I grow gradually better: much however remains to mend." And he adds the supplication in Greek, Κύριε ἐλέησον, "Lord have mercy."

The most portentous Greek entry however occurs in his Diary of a journey into Wales (1774). Under date of August 14, two Greek words βρῶσις ὀλίγη significantly stand of themselves; and being rendered into homely English reveal "short commons." The first editor of the Diary, commenting upon them, infers that "on that day Johnson ate sparingly." No doubt; for he could not have helped himself. And unless Duppa put forward that inference by way of charitable interpretation, his knowledge of Greek must have been as beggarly as the victuals to which Johnson was then reduced by some inhospitable host. As a matter of fact, the Doctor indignantly records, in suitably severe Laconics, the Spartan fare provided for him on that inauspicious occasion.

The Diary bristles with Greek thoughts and Greek allusions. At Lleweney he dined with his old friend Dr. Shipley, the Bishop of St. Asaph, and there was "talk of Greek." On that day (August 8) Johnson "read Phocylides, and distinguished the paragraphs";

DR. JOHNSON AS A GRECIAN

meaning evidently that he made out the sections, each treating of a special subject. He does not appear however to have suspected that this didactic poem, "the title of which (as Duppa is careful to note) is Ποίημα Νουθετικὸν," but which is also known as Φωκυλίδου ἀργυρᾶ ἔπη and Φωκυλίδου γνῶμαι, is a Pseudophocylidean forgery of Christian times. On the way back to London Blenheim was visited, and Dr. Johnson notes in his Diary: "Mr. Bryant showed me the Library with great civility." He singles out two of the rarest Greek books, the "Batrachomyomachia"—the first portion of the Homeric poems ever printed (Venice, 1486)—and Lascaris' Grammar, issued just ten years earlier at Milan. This grammar is the first book printed entirely in Greek types, as Dr. Johnson is careful to note in another column of the Diary, and only four or five copies of it are known to exist now. The particular copy in question was acquired, at the sale of the famous Sunderland Library, for a German bibliophile, who, however, demurred to the exorbitant price. But I, in my earlier enthusiasm, readily offered the sum, and the precious volume is now in my possession.

Another entry in the Diary is the following:—"I read in the morning Wasse's Greek Trochaics to Bentley. They appeared inelegant and made with difficulty. . . . The Greek I did not always fully understand. I am in doubt about the sixth and last paragraphs; perhaps they are not printed right; for εὔτοκον perhaps εὔστοχον." His criticism is sound, but the proposed emendation unnecessary. Εὔτοκον stands as applied to a productive mind.[1]

In a preceding entry Johnson tries his hand at Greek epigram, the subject of which proves that his projected "History of the Revival of Learning in Europe" still lurked in his mind.

"Τὸ πρῶτον Μῶρος, τὸ δὲ δεύτερον εἷλεν Ἔρασμος,
Τὸ τρίτον ἐκ Μουσῶν στέμμα Μίκυλλος ἔχει."[2]

("More won the first, Erasmus the second, Micyllus has the third crown from the Muses.") Sir Thomas More's pre-eminence among his contemporaries as a Greek scholar is indisputable, and Johnson refers to him in high terms on other occasions; Moltzer also was a distinguished Greek scholar.[3] But it is strange that

[1] Duppa and those after him throw no light on the subject. Dr. G. B. Hill indexes Wasse as Christopher. His Christian name was Joseph. He is known as commentator on Thucydides and Sallust, and was a fellow of Queen's College. Bentley said of him, "When I am dead Wasse will be the most learned man in England." But he preceded Bentley by nearly four years. He was the chief contributor to the "Bibliotheca Literaria," which, under the editorship of Dr. Sam Jebb, ran into ten numbers between 1722-24. At p. 9 of No. vi. occur Wasse's fifty Greek lines in praise of Bentley and his Horace.

[2] Duppa notes: "In the MS. Johnson has introduced ᾔρεν (sic) by the side of εἷλεν." Both Duppa's Greek quotations and those of other editors of Boswell are full of faults in accentuation, such as appear to be inevitable where Greek is pronounced only by quantity.

[3] "Much credit is due to the first translators of Greek authors; Grævius and Benedictus give place to Sir Thomas More among all the translators of Lucian" (Croker, p. 837).—Jacobus Moltzer, b. 1503, was surnamed Micyllus when he played that rôle in Lucian's "Somnium," which was dramatised at the Gymnasium of Frankfort. He translated Lucian into Latin (1538), edited Homer with Scholia (1541), became

DR. JOHNSON AS A GRECIAN

Johnson's critical acumen should have failed him in regard to Erasmus, whose knowledge of Greek was of the thinnest and shallowest, and was justly scorned by his French contemporary, the illustrious Budæus. This proves, however, how much a prig, a trimmer, and a "farceur," such as Erasmus undoubtedly was, can accomplish in securing for himself a "reputation usurpée," warranted to last several generations.

It was on his first visit to Blenheim, just referred to, or, perhaps, on his second with Boswell in 1776, that Johnson must have been moved to render into Greek the Abbé Salvini's Latin epigram on John Duke of Marlborough ("Works," I. p. 191) :—

> "Haud alio vultu fremuit Mars acer in armis ;
> Haud alio Cypriam percutit ore Deam."

> "Τοῖος Ἄρης βροτολοιγὸς ἐνὶ πολέμοισι μέμηνε,
> Καὶ τοῖος Παφίην πλῆξεν ἔρωτι θεάν."

On another occasion he composed the following on his friend, the Rev. Dr. Thomas Birch ("Works," I. p. 170 :—

> "Εἶπεν Ἀληθείη πρώην χαίρουσα γράφοντα
> Ἡρώων τε βίους Βίρχιον ἠδὲ σοφῶν.
> Καὶ βίον, εἶπεν, ὅταν ῥίψῃς θανάτοιο βέλεσσι
> Σοῦ ποτε γραψόμενον Βίρχιον ἄλλον ἔχοις."

And in his letter to Langton, in which the Κύριε ἐλέησον occurs, he says : "I wrote the following tetrastick on poor Goldsmith :—

Rector of the Gymnasium in 154-, and subsequently held the chair of Greek at Heidelberg, where he died in 1558.

"'Τὸν τάφον εἰσοράᾳς τὸν Ὀλιβαρίοιο, κονίην
Ἄφρασι μὴ σεμνήν, ξεῖνε, πώτεσσι πάτει.
Οἷσι μέμηλε φύσις, μέτρων χάρις, ἔργα παλαιῶν,
Κλαίετε ποιητήν, ἱστορικόν, φυσικόν.'"

It is an epitaph full of classic solemnity and grace, of which Mr. Seward ("Anec." ii. p. 466) gives the following translation:—

> "Whoe'er thou art, with reverence tread
> Where Goldsmith's letter'd dust is laid.
> If nature and the historic page,
> If the sweet muse thy care engage,
> Lament him dead whose powerful mind
> Their various energies combined."

In another letter, to Mr. Cave, Johnson writes: "I have composed a Greek epigram to Eliza, and think she ought to be celebrated in as many different languages as Lewis le Grand." The epigram in question, with a Latin version, is inserted in "Works," I. p. 170.

ΕΙΣ ΤΟ ΤΗΣ ΕΛΙΣΣΗΣ ΠΕΡΙ ΤΩΝ ΟΝΕΙΡΩΝ ΑΙΝΙΓΜΑ.

Τῇ κάλλους ἐνάμει τί τέλος; Ζεὺς πάντα ἔδωκεν
Κύπριδι, μηδ' αὐτοῦ σκῆπτρα μέμηλε Θεῷ.
Ἐκ Διὸς ἐστιν ὄναρ, θειός ποτ' ἔγραψεν Ὅμηρος,
Ἀλλὰ τόδ' εἰς θνητοὺς Κύπρις ἔπεμψεν ὄναρ.
Ζεὺς μοῦνος φλογόεντι πόλεις ἔπερσε κεραυνῷ,
Ὄμμασι λαμπρὰ Διὸς Κύπρις ὦστα φέρει.

This was the famous Mrs. Elizabeth Carter, whose attainments he esteemed so highly that even of Langton he said "that he understood Greek better than any one whom he had ever known, except Elizabeth Carter." In fact, he recognised in her an exception to the rule he himself had laid down in respect to the scholarly training of the fair sex.[1]

Hawkins relates that Johnson, upon hearing a lady commended for her learning, said: "A man is in general better pleased when he has a good dinner upon his table than when his wife talks Greek. My old friend, Mrs. Carter, would make a pudding as well as translate Epictetus."[2]

Johnson's reverence for Greek learning was such that proficiency in the language immediately raised a man in his consideration. Of Mr. Longley, father of Archbishop Longley, and Recorder of Rochester, whom he met there, he said, "My heart warms towards him. I was surprised to find in him such a nice acquaintance with the metre in the learned languages; though I was somewhat mortified that I had it not so much to myself as I should have thought." Mr. Longley, however, modestly explains that the impression he made upon Johnson was by a mere fluke.

[1] Johnson's opinion on the social status of the sex is clearly set forth in a letter to Taylor, first published by the Philobiblon Society: "Nature," he says, "has given women so much power that the law has very wisely given them little." He was, nevertheless, ready to encourage and assist another lady in her literary pursuits. To the English version of the Greek Theatre of Father Brumoy, which Mrs. Ch. Lennox published in 1759, Dr. Johnson contributed the translation of "A Dissertation on the Greek Comedy," and "The General Conclusion of the Book."

[2] All the Works of Epictetus which are now extant, containing his Discourses, preserved by Arrian in four books, the Enchiridon and Fragments. Translated from the original Greek by Elizabeth Carter, with an Introduction and Notes. London, 1788. 4°. (In the list of subscribers the name of "S. Johnson, M.A.," occurs.)

"Had he examined me further, I fear he could have found me ignorant."[1] And he adds, about Langton his neighbour, that he "was a very good Greek scholar, much superior to Johnson, to whom, nevertheless, he paid profound deference; sometimes, indeed, I thought more than he deserved."

Bennet Langton's qualities and attainments were many and various, and all such as to impress Johnson deeply. The tall Lincolnshire squire, "resembling a stork standing on one leg near the shore in Raphael's cartoon of the Miraculous Draught of Fishes" (and hence nicknamed Lanky), was a man of that ancient lineage and those polished manners which fascinated Johnson; while his sincere piety and his equable and entertaining conversation endeared him to the Doctor. Johnson writes (June 1, 1728) to Th. Warton, Langton's tutor at Oxford: "His mind is as exalted as his stature. I am half afraid of him; but he is no less amiable than formidable." And again he said: "The earth does not bear a worthier man than Bennet Langton. . . . I know not who will go to heaven if Langton does not. Sir, I will almost say, *sit anima mea cum Langtono.*"

But it was Langton's knowledge of Greek which completely subjugated Johnson. It was not, what may be styled the pedantic, nor the mercenary know-

---

[1] The passage from Longley's unpublished "Autobiography" is quoted by Dr. G. Birkbeck Hill (iv. p. 8), to whose monumental edition of "The Life" I am greatly indebted.

DR. JOHNSON AS A GRECIAN

ledge of the language, acquired as a means to ostentation or gain. Langton loved Greek for its own sake; he felt its beauty; he was imbued with the charm of its literature and the ennobling influence of its godlike grandeur, so that he came to live and think in it, and even crack jokes in Greek. When he first met Johnson he took him by storm. He had read a good deal in Clenardus's Greek Grammar. "Why, sir," said Johnson, "who is there in this town who knows anything of Clenardus but you and I?" Clenardus's Grammar, although at that time superannuated, had long held the field and had gone through as many editions in the West as George Gennadius's Greek Grammar is still being issued in Greece and the East. But Langton had also learned by heart the whole of the Epistle of St. Basil, which is given in that grammar as *praxis*. "Sir," said Johnson in wrapt admiration, "I never made such an effort to attain Greek."

Langton's ready command of Greek is attested by Miss L. M. Hawkins,[1] who writes: "He would get into the most fluent recitation of half a page of Greek, breaking off for fear of wearying, by saying, as I well remember his phrase, 'and so it goes on,' accompanying his words with a gentle wave of his hand, indicating that you might better suppose the rest than bear his proceeding." Langton would nevertheless enjoy a liberty taken with his beloved Greek, and one evening,

[1] "Memoirs, Anecdotes," &c. London, 1824. 2 vols.

as Boswell writes, "made us laugh heartily at some lines by Joshua Barnes, in which are to be found such comical Anglo-Hellenisms as κλύϐϐοισιν ἴϐαγχθεν— they were banged with clubs." Among his other classical witticisms were macaronic Greek verses, such as "Fivepoundon elendeto; ah! mala simplos." In all this he was no doubt aided by his constant reading of Aristophanes, to whom he was so devoted that even Johnson's urgings, that he should neglect Aristophanes rather than his material interests, was of no avail.

Equally ineffectual proved Johnson's preference for pudding-making over proficiency in Greek for women. Miss Hawkins says that Langton told her father "that he should not only give his sons, but his daughters, a knowledge of the learned languages, and that he meant to familiarise the latter with the Greek language to such perfection, that while five of his girls employed themselves in feminine works, the sixth should read a Greek author for the general amusement." Langton, you see, like a good Englishman, had girls by the half-dozen; there were ten living, I believe; some, however, were boys.

He determined that the elder of these, George, should learn also Modern Greek—an undreamt of acquirement in those days; and with a prophetic insight into the future, he engaged as tutor one Lucignan, a Levantine claimant, I presume, of the name and heritage of the Frank Kings of Cyprus.

DR. JOHNSON AS A GRECIAN

Lucignan, who appears to have been as accomplished a courtier as he was a good Catholic, declared one day that his director had imposed upon him, as a penance, to recite a certain number of times, before breakfast (and in eager anticipation of the meal) the words Κύριε Ἐλέησον —the very words which Johnson, when troubled with bodily suffering, had used in his letter to Langton. So Lucignan paced up and down his room, loudly repeating his *Kyrielle* (as the French style it), but, like a thoughtful man, opened his door now and anon, calling downstairs to the maid, "Is my breakfast ready?" Dr. Johnson must have been just then a guest at Langton's.

But where did Langton get his notion about Modern Greek? Search for the Greek who, like the Scotchman, is sure to turn up, always and everywhere. In a letter to Boswell (May 21, 1775) Johnson writes: "Mr. Langton went yesterday to Lincolnshire, and has invited Nicolaida to follow him." And again in his "Prayers and Meditations" (March 18, 1782): "I rose late, looked a little into books, saw Mrs. Reynolds and Miss Thrale and Nicolaida. I then dined on tea." (Another unsatisfactory meal!)

And who was this Nicolaida? Boswell, in a note, describes him as "a learned Greek"; and in Johnson's "Life of Dr. Parr" (I. p. 84) we read: "With Mr. Paradise, who had been the British Consul at Salonichi, he (Parr) became acquainted through Sir William Jones, and also with Mr. Nicolaides, a learned Greek, nephew of the Patriarch of Constantinople, who fled from some massacre of the Greeks." The name is here given correctly, Nicolaid*es*, not Nicolaid*a*; and there follow (pp. 87-90) two letters from him to Dr. Parr, the one in excellent classic Greek and full of Greek erudition, justifying his description as "a learned Greek"; the other in quaint and mis-spelt English, with this P.S. : "Jonson is gon to france with Mr. and Mrs. Threile and Mr. Beretti."[1]

I am proud to think that at that time a countryman and a precursor of mine to these shores enjoyed the friendship and daily converse of Dr. Johnson and of the gentle Bennet Langton. He was a man of birth and culture, and a refugee from one of the periodical outbreaks of savagery of the unspeakable Turk. It was, no doubt, his presence as a refugee that moved the Doctor to remark, "Alexander the Great swept India, now the Turks sweep Greece"; although Johnson had already, in his "Irene," given expression to his warm sympathy with the enslaved race. It was Nicolaides's use of Greek as his living mother tongue that must have added to Johnson's ardour for the

---

[1] I am indebted to Dr. G. B. Hill for the following extract from Mrs. Delany's "Autobiography and Correspondence," v. 248. Writing from Bulstrod, the home of the Dowager-Duchess of Portland, on August 5, 1776, she says :—"In the evening came the renowned Mr. Burke—take him out of politics and he is very entertaining—he brought a Monsieur Nicolaide, a Grecian, who was full of silent admiration."

DR JOHNSON AS A GRECIAN

noble language. So that, we are told, even at the close of his life, "during his sleepless nights, he amused himself by translating into Latin verse, from the Greek, many of the epigrams of the 'Anthologia.'"[1]

Johnson, as we have seen, was from the very first enamoured with these sweet flowers of Greek literature —soothing by their fragrance and enchanting in their varied hues. On August 8, 1772, he wrote to Boswell: "You promised to get me a little *Pindar :* you may add to it a little *Anacreon.*" And again in February, 1782, "When you come hither, pray bring with you Baxter's *Anacreon.* I cannot get that edition in London." And he repeated his request on March 18, 1784: "Please to bring with you Baxter's 'Anacreon.'" But Boswell's father apparently would not let the rare volume go. Johnson had not seen it till he visited Auchinleck. "Dr. Johnson found here Baxter's 'Anacreon' which he told me (writes Boswell) he had long inquired for in vain, and began to suspect there was no such book. My father has written many notes on this book, and Dr. Johnson and I talked of having it reprinted."[2] In like manner with other

---

[1] He himself wrote to Mrs. Piozzi on April 19, 1784: "When I lay sleepless I used to drive the night along by turning Greek epigrams into Latin. I know not if I have not turned a hundred." There are just over ninety reprinted in his "Works," I. 175-179. He had before him the text of Budæus, Basil, 1549.

[2] 'Ανακρέοντος Μέλη. Pluribus quibus hæctanus scatebant mendis purgavit ... notarque ... adjecit. W. Baxter. Londini, 1695.— Ed. Altera, Londini, 1710. 8°. Boswell writing to Johnson, says that "Baxter's 'Anacreon' which is in the library at Auchinleck, was, I find,

Greek poets. In his "Meditations" (1773) he refers to the "Argonautica" as a daily reading of his.[1] "How goes Appollonius?" he inquires (May 13, 1765) of Mr. Warton, who was preparing a translation. And with the concluding verse of Dionysius's Periegesis he brings to an end the last number of "The Rambler."

> "Αὐτῶν ἐκ μακάρων ἀντάξιος εἴη ἀμοιβή."
> "Celestial powers! that piety regard,
> From you my labours wait their last reward."

It is that verse—but distorted and maimed to suit the narrow evangelicalism of Sir W. Scott; jumbled together to look like an ancient inscription, as pompous old Dr. Parr imagined[2]—it is that same Greek verse we may now read on the scroll of his effigy at St. Paul's Cathedral:—

> "Ἐν μακάρεσσι πόνων ἀντάξιος εἴη ἀμοιβή."

---

collated by my father in 1727 with the MS. belonging to the University of Leyden, and he has made a number of notes upon it. Would you advise me to publish a new edition of it?" His answer was dated Sept. 30 (1783). . . . "Your 'Anacreon' is a very uncommon book. Whether it should be reprinted, you cannot do better than consult Lord Hailes."

[1] "L. Apollonii pugnam Betriciam." Dr. G. B. Hill explains ("Johnsonian Miscel.," I. 69) that in Apollonius's Argonautica, bk. ii., there is the description of a fight between Polydeuces and Amycus, King of the Bebryces, which Johnson may have Latinised as *pugna Bebrycia* or *Bebricia*, and this may have been misprinted as *Betricia*.

[2] An amusing, but unedifying correspondence (covering no less than thirty-six pages in vol. iv. of Dr. Parr's "Works") in which Sir J. Reynolds, Sir W. Scott, Malone, Burney, and Seward joined, furnishes an account of the debate waged over this question. It must be admitted that Parr pointed out the unreasonableness of the change insisted upon.

DR. JOHNSON AS A GRECIAN

To the last he prided himself on his Greek. With his Greek learning he taught; with his Greek erudition he battled; with his Greek lore he repelled attack. When a ludicrous paragraph appeared in the newspapers that he was receiving lessons in dancing from Madame Vestris, and he was asked sarcastically if it was true, he told them they might reply:—
"Why should Dr. Johnson not add to his other powers a little corporal agility? Socrates learned to dance at an advanced age, and Cato learnt Greek at an advanced age." And when, lounging on the Scottish shore, he was hurriedly invited to embark, for the wind was fair and Skipper Simpson's boat ready to sail, with composure and solemnity he repeated that grand passage in Epictetus, in which we are warned that, "as man has the voyage of death before him, whatever may be his employment, he should be ready at the Master's call; and an old man should never be far from the shore, lest he should not be able to get himself ready."[1] The supreme moment

---

[1] The editors of "The Life" have not identified this passage. It is evidently Johnson's (or Boswell's) recollection of Mrs. Carter's rather awkwardly worded version of the seventh chapter of the Enchiridion. "As in a voyage, when the ship is at anchor, if you go on shore to get water, you may amuse yourself with picking up a shell-fish [shell] or an onion [sic! say rather a bulb, such as abound on the shores of Greece] in your way; but your thoughts ought to be bent towards the ship and perpetually attentive, lest the captain should call; and then you must leave all these things, that you may not be thrown into the vessel bound neck and heels, like a sheep. Thus likewise in life, if instead of an onion or a shell-fish, such a thing as a wife or a child be granted you, there is no objection; but if the captain call, run to the ship, leave all

when we are to exchange time for eternity, seemed, by the superb exhortation of the Greek philosopher, to be for once bereft of dread for Doctor Johnson.

Thus, inured in life-long struggles, fortified in spirit by a robust faith, exalted in mind by the loftiest expression of Greek philosophy, Johnson was one of those few who are numbered among the immortals while still in this life: even as that other great Englishman and greatest of modern men, whom the world has just mourned with you, but whom Immortality now claims as one of her noblest ornaments.

these things, regard none of them. But if you are old, never go far from the ship; lest, when you are called you should be unable to come in time."—Johnson had a just appreciation of the philosophy of Epictetus, which, in its loftiness and purity, is but little inferior to the teaching of our Saviour; so much so that for many centuries the Discourses and the Enchiridion were in daily use in Greek monasteries. It is, therefore, not surprising to find among Johnson's metrical renderings the following tetrastich, inscribed "Epictetus."

> " Me, rex deorum, tuque, duc, necessitas,
> Quo, lege vestra, vita me feret mea.
> Sequar libenter, sin reluctari velim,
> Fiam scelestus, nec tamen minus sequar."

BOSWELL'S PROOF-SHEETS

A Paper read before the Johnson Club
BY
GEORGE BIRKBECK HILL, D.C.L., LL.D.

Honorary Fellow of Pembroke College, Oxford

(*First published in "The Atlantic Monthly"*)

JAMES BOSWELL, AFTER SIR JOSHUA REYNOLDS.

[To face p. 51.

Boswell's Proof-Sheets

In the summer of 1893 I spent nearly three months in the pleasant village of Barnstable, on Cape Cod, with an Italian sky above my head, and a sea blue as the Mediterranean stretching out before me. For some days I had an occupation so little likely to befall any one in so out-of-the way a spot that I never lost the feeling of its delightful incongruity. That I, an English scholar, should take up my abode there seemed strange enough. That I should there be reading the proof-sheets of the first edition of the " Life of Johnson," and be copying the corrections made on them in Boswell's clear, large hand, seemed almost a marvel. Even Johnson, who would scarcely allow that anything was extraordinary, aware as he was of " the natural desire of man to propagate a wonder," would have owned that here there was something greatly out of the common. If the country folk, as they passed to and fro, had known what I was doing, as I sat under the wide verandah, and had been able to understand all the strangeness of the circumstances, they would surely have gazed at me with wonder. There was an old gentleman of the village who, eighty years before, when sailing with his father in the Cape Cod and Boston packet, had been captured by an English frigate. I wished that he had chanced to drop in when I had the proofs open at the passage where Johnson, "breathing out threatening and slaughter" against the Americans "roared out a tremendous volley which one might fancy could be heard across the Atlantic." It would have added still more to the sense of incongruity.

There often came into my mind "the sudden air of exultation" with which, a few months before his death, at a meeting of his club, Johnson exclaimed, "Oh! gentlemen, I must tell you a very great thing. The Empress of Russia has ordered 'The Rambler' to be translated into the Russian language; so I shall be read on the banks of the Volga. Horace boasts that his fame would extend as far as the banks of the Rhone; now the Volga is farther from me than the Rhone was from Horace." When he was shown over Keddlestone, Lord Scarsdale's country seat, finding in his lordship's dressing-room a copy of his Dictionary, "he showed it to me with some eagerness," writes Boswell, "saying 'Lookye! *Quæ regio in terris nostri non plena laboris?*' He observed also Goldsmith's 'Animated Nature,' and said, 'Here's our friend! The poor doctor would have been happy to hear of this.'" How widely are the works of genius scattered! In the frozen ocean, on the shores of King William Island, a copy of the "Vicar of Wakefield" was found in a boat by the side of the skeletons of two of Franklin's sailors. My proof-sheets came to me on Cape Cod from the very borders of Canada—that "region of desolate sterility," to use Johnson's own description, "from which nothing but furs and fish were to be had." To these borders Goldsmith had led his "pensive exile":

> "Where wild Oswego spreads her swamps around,
> And Niagara stuns with thund'ring sound.
> . . . .
> Where beasts with man divided empire claim,
> And the brown Indian marks with murderous aim."

There on the shore of Lake Erie and on the banks of Niagara, a nobler river than either the Rhone or the Volga, in the flourishing town of Buffalo, I had found a finer collection of Johnsonian and Boswellian curiosities than exists anywhere on our side of the Atlantic. There were not only first editions of all the works and ten or twelve original letters of the two men, but in addition a large and most interesting collection of autographs, portraits, and engravings in illustration of my editions of the "Life and Letters of Johnson." Whoever was mentioned in the text or in the notes of either of these works, from Burke and Reynolds, Goldsmith and Garrick, downwards, of him, if they could be found, a likeness and an autograph letter had been procured. The devout Johnsonian, after visiting Lichfield, Pembroke College, and Fleet

Street, after following the great man's footsteps in Scotland, will henceforth have to cross the Atlantic and end his pilgrimage on the pleasant shores of Lake Erie. From Mr. R. B. Adam, the liberal owner of these treasures, he may count on receiving a warm welcome. Let him prove his title to *Johnsonianissimus*, and the shrine will be thrown open to him. I shall never join in the lament that is raised among us Englishmen when the autographs and rare editions of our great writers are bought by an American. Each becomes a link to bind its new owner to the old country; each reminds him that he too is of the great English stock; each makes him

> "Cast a long look where England's glories shine,
> And bids his bosom sympathise with mine."

Great as has been the liberality of some of our collectors in letting me see their stores, Mr. Adam, in his liberality, has far surpassed them all. A fresh proof of this I was to receive soon after my arrival at Barnstable. A few weeks after I had taken leave of him he acquired, at a cost of one hundred and forty-seven pounds, Boswell's proof-sheets. These he sent me by post. I was to keep them as long as I needed. They were shortly followed by Johnson's proof-sheets of his "Life of Pope," with the corrections in his own writing. How unlike it is to Boswell's big hand! yet it does not deserve the description which Hawkesworth gave of it to one of his correspondents. "Take," he wrote, "his own testimony in his own words; they are written, indeed, not in letters but in pothooks, a kind of character which it will probably cost you some time to decipher, and perhaps at last you may not succeed."

I had once tried to penetrate into Auchinleck, Boswell's ancestral home. I had hoped, in the library where his father and Johnson "came into collision over Oliver Cromwell's coin," to find many curious memorials. Permission was refused me. My attempt even excited suspicion; for soon after I had made it I received the following letter, which, now that the venerable writer is dead, may without impropriety be given to the world. "I hope," wrote Boswell, in the preface of his "Account of Corsica," "that if this work should at any future period be republished care will be taken of my orthography." This pious care I have taken of the orthography of his granddaughter.

"44 QUEEN STREET, EDINBURGH,
"*June* 1, 1889.

"DEAR SIR,—I am told you are about to publish another addition of My Grandfathers book—'Boswell's, Life of Johnston,' and that you have 'some papers from Ayrshire'! May I ask you to be so good as inform me from whom you received them and oblige
"Yours faithfully
"M. E. VASSALL.

"I may tell you that I am daughter of Sir Alexander Boswell."

The letter was addressed to "G. Berbick Hill, Esq."

I could scarcely complain of her not knowing that my "addition" of Boswell had been published full two years when she wrote, or of her misspelling my name, when *Johnson* was changed by her into *Johnston*. "Are you of the Johnstons of Glencro or of Ardnamurchan?" the Laird of Lochbuy bawled out to him when he was visiting his castle on the Island of Mull. Dr. Johnson gave him a significant look, but made no answer. Mrs. Vassall's contemptuous ignorance of the great man's name came to her from her father. "I have observed," wrote Sir Walter Scott, "he disliked any allusion to 'The Life' or to Johnson himself, and I have heard that Johnson's fine picture by Sir Joshua was sent upstairs out of the sitting apartments at Auchinleck." He was killed in a duel seventy-two years ago. Scott lamented his fall, and Jeffrey defended his adversary when he was put on his trial. His daughter died but a year or two ago. So unexpectedly near were brought these "unhappy far-off things." Her only brother, Sir James Boswell, shared in the prejudices of his family. An elderly lady, who was his guest at Auchinleck, told me that one day, when the talk fell on his race-horses, he said that he did not know what name to give one of them. She suggested Boswell's Johnsoniana, "which made him very angry."

BOSWELL'S PROOF-SHEETS

That which was refused me on the spot where Boswell " walked among the rocks and woods of his ancestors with an agreeable consciousness that he had done something worthy " was granted me on Cape Cod. May more of our old libraries fall under the auctioneer's hammer, and more of our collections be carried across the Atlantic, provided that they come into the hands of citizens as enlightened and liberal as my friend Mr. R. B. Adam.

Interesting and curious as these proofs are, they would have been still more interesting and still more curious had they been the first which Boswell corrected, and not mere revises. Doubtless many a passage was modified, many an insertion and many an omission made, when he first went through his task. Nevertheless, even in this revision there is a good gleaning to be made. To recover the passages on two cancelled pages is in itself no small triumph. It is a pleasant thing, moreover, to be admitted as it were into Boswell's study, and to see him at work as he corrects the book which is to make his name famous wherever the English tongue is spoken. He is, on the whole, on good terms with his compositors, though he now and then shows an author's impatience at the slowness of the press. " I request a little more despatch," he wrote on one sheet. A few sheets later on, he entered: " This is very well done indeed. Pray, gentlemen compositors, let me have as much as you can before Christmas."

"Mr. Compositor," said Johnson on one occasion, "Mr. Compositor, I ask your pardon again and again." But this was when, without any just cause, he had sent for the man in a passion. Boswell's complimentary language is clearly for the sake of putting the compositors into good humour. On September 20, 1790, nearly half the book was in type. On March 4th of the following year he wrote on the last sheet but five: "I hope by Monday to have *all the remaining copy in the Printing House.* If possible let us be *out* this month." It was not till May 16th, the twenty-eighth anniversary of the day on which he first met Johnson, that the immortal biography, the *Magnum Opus*, as he used to call it, was published. A delay was sometimes caused by his desire " to ascertain particulars with a scrupulous authenticity." "Sheet yyy," he wrote, " is with Mr. Wilkes to look at a note." The note contains " the *sentimental anecdote* with which Mr. Wilkes with his usual readiness pleasantly matched " one of Baretti's stories.[1] A short delay is caused in ascertaining the number of years the Rev. Mr. Vilette had been Ordinary of Newgate. A blank had been left in the text. On the margin Boswell wrote: "Send my note to Mr. Vilette in the morning and open the answer. Or inquire of Mr. Akerman (the keeper of Newgate, "my esteemed friend," as he called him) for the number of years. Get it somehow." To a man who

[1] See the Clarendon Press edition of my " Boswell's Life of Johnson," iv. 347.

had Boswell's morbid love of seeing the hangman do his work, accuracy on such a point was of great importance, for almost every year of the reverend gentleman's spiritual duties was marked by his attendance at a score or two of executions at least. On page 505 of the second volume Boswell writes: "I could wish that the forme in which page 512 is were not thrown off till I have an answer from Mr. Stone, the gentleman mentioned in the note, to tell me his Christian name, that I may call him Esq." Mr. Stone, it seems, did not reply, for "Mr. Stone" he remained, and still remains, in all subsequent editions. In Boswell's eyes there was a great difference between *Esq.* and *Mr.* "You would observe," he wrote to Malone, "some stupid lines on Mr. Burke in the Oracle *by Mr. Boswell.* Sir William Scott told me I could have no legal redress. So I went *civilly* to Bell, and he promised to mention *handsomely* that *James Boswell, Esq.* was not the author of the lines." His rival biographer he described as "Mr. John Hawkins, an attorney," in return for the description which Hawkins had given of him as "Mr. James Boswell, a native of Scotland." To Hawkins himself he had complained of the slight thus put upon him. "Well, but *Mr. James Boswell,* surely, surely, *Mr. James Boswell.*"

He now and then reproaches his compositors. *Stephani* had been printed *Stephen.* "Don't you know the Stephani the famous Printers?" he wrote on the margin. "You do not put a semicolon often enough. Pray attend to this," he entered on another sheet. The reproof, he reflects, is not just, so he adds, "But it is *my duty* to point. So I have no right to find fault." In the margin of the passage in which he quotes the inscription on a gold snuff-box given to Reynolds by Catherine II., he writes, "Pray be very careful in printing the words of the Empress of *all the Russias*." There is, nevertheless, an error in the French, due probably to Boswell, who, though he was Secretary for Foreign Correspondence to the Royal Academy, was but a poor French scholar. Opposite the long note where he praises the anonymous editor of "Tracts by Warburton and a Warburtonian" he writes in the margin, "*This page* must not be laid on till I hear from Dr. Parr whether his name may be mentioned." Accordingly, he wrote to him requesting "to hear by return of post if I may say or guess that Dr. Parr is the editor." Apparently the letter was not answered, or else permission was refused, though the authorship could not have been a secret. Parr's name does not appear in the note. Boswell was more fortunate in obtaining a name for another entry, which had originally stood, "He was in this like ―――, who, Mr. Daines Barrington told me, used to say, 'I hate a *cui bono* man.'" In the margin he filled up the blank with "a respectable person"; but before the sheet was "laid on" he learnt this respectable person's name. In the published text he figures as "Dr. Shaw, the great traveller."

BOSWELL'S PROOF-SHEETS

Quoting Johnson's published letter to Mrs. Thrale about the Gordon Riots, he gives the spelling *jails*, as she had given it. The "reader" queries *gaols*. Boswell replies, "Either way, *jails* or *gaols* is in his Dictionary." Two pages further on, where the word recurs, the "reader" rejoins, "Dr. Johnson in his Dictionary says jail is an improper way of spelling gaol." Johnson, under *gaol*, writes, "It is always pronounced, and too often written *jail* and sometimes *gaol*." The "reader" has his way, and it is *gaols* in the text. Boswell hesitates over the word *divines*, in a passage where he had described a letter to a young clergyman as containing "valuable advice to divines in general." For *divines* he first substituted *Parish priests*, but at last added, "Stet Divines but with D cap." He rejoices in the result of all the care which he takes. "How lucky it is that I have had this Revise!" he enters on the first sheet. "*Franly* for *frankly* would have looked ill. I trust we shall have a *very* correct book." Later on he records, "By revising this sheet again I have catched an Island which I had omitted." The island was Inchkenneth, about the spelling of which he thus warns the compositor: "Pray observe that in Inchkenneth there is first an H and then a K. As these letters are apt to be mistaken in M. S., I mention this. The first syllable of the word is the same with the measure Inch." On another proof he writes, "I am sorry that there must be a little over, running on in this sheet. But we must make as good a Book as may be." On the top of almost every sheet, from the first to the last, he enters, "For Press when carefully looked at by Mr. Selfe, and corrected."

The "reader" sometimes suggests a doubt or a correction. He does not like the repetition where Johnson says, "We may be excused for not caring much about other people's children, for there are many who care very little about their own children." He would strike out the last word. Boswell replies, "The repetition is the Johnsonian mode." Miss Hawkins, in her "Memoirs," mentions this "Johnsonian mode." "In this way," she writes, "I heard him take the part of Sir Matthew Hale, saying, 'If Hale had anything to say, let Hale say it.'" The "reader" queried *senility*. "A good word," Boswell replied. It is not, however, in Johnson's Dictionary. "Aversion *from* entails" was objected to. Boswell would not admit the objection. "It is," he wrote, "right as in Johnson's letter. Averse *from* is legitimate language." In his Dictionary Johnson says that "averse *to*" is "very frequently but improperly used." Dr. Murray gives lists of eminent writers who have used, some one construction, some the other, and some both. In the margin of Johnson's Greek lines on Goldsmith the "reader" notes: "The accents are very wrong. Would it be better to omit them? If you choose to keep them, I will take care of them." Boswell replies: "I leave it optional to you to have accents or not. Mr. Thomas Warton used none." A kind of compromise seems to have been arrived at: all the accents were removed but two.

Many of the corrections are curious. Thus, where Johnson, speaking of "a gentleman of his acquaintance," said, "I should be apt to throw******'s verses in his face," in the proof, instead of the six asterisks, there was a simple dash. Boswell, it is clear, made this change so that the minor poet might be recognised by his friends. William Seward, I conjecture, was the man. A few pages further on, he objects to the dash which stands for George the Second. "Make the — a little longer," he writes. In the second edition he has three dashes given, so that it may be more clearly seen who was the king who destroyed his father's will. He now and then suppresses a name. In Johnson's diary of his tour in France an entry had been printed, "At D'Argenson's I looked into the books in the lady's closet, and in contempt shewed them to Mr. T." Boswell writes, "As the word is not quite clear, and it is at any rate more polite not to name the Lady, make it thus, At D———'s." Instead of the dash eight asterisks were substituted in the second edition, whence the name was easily conjectured; for "Mr. Argenson" had been mentioned just before. Boswell was, I suspect, capable of suppressing a name because he disliked a man. At the end of the account of the altercation between Johnson and Beauclerk he had at first written,

"Dr. Johnson with Mr. Steevens sat with him a long time after the rest of the company were gone." In later years he had more than once suffered from Steevens's malignity, and so, I surmise, would not let him have the honour of being thus distinguished. He substituted for his name "another gentleman." His dislike of Gibbon was sufficiently expressed in the text as he published it. "Mr. Gibbon," he writes, "with his usual sneer controverted it, perhaps in resentment of Johnson's having talked with some disgust of his ugliness, which one would think a *philosopher* would not mind." To this passage he added in the margin, after Gibbon's name, "the historical writer, and to me offensive sneerer at what I hold sacred." The addition was not made. Boswell probably was persuaded out of it. A little more respect was shown to the great writer in the correction of the proof of the Index, where he had appeared as "Gibbon, the historian." This was changed by Boswell into "Gibbon, Edward, Esq." In the same place an addition was made to the entry about Alexander Wedderburne, Lord Loughborough, whose rapid rise Boswell envied. It had stood, "Loughborough, Lord, his great good fortune." After "his" was inserted "talents and." Thurlow is treated as unceremoniously as Steevens. In 1785, in "A Letter addressed to the People of Scotland," Boswell informed them that "now that Dr. Johnson is gone to a better world he [Boswell] bowed the intellectual knee to

Lord Thurlow." In the proof-sheets there was a fine compliment to his lordship in the passage where Boswell attempts to pay "a suitable tribute of admiration" to Warren Hastings. "But how weak," he wrote, "would be my voice after that of a Thurlow." The last two words he changed into "the millions whom he governed." If Thurlow was thus slighted by the correction on this sheet, Johnson was magnified. Boswell had spoken of Hastings as "a man whose regard reflects consequence even upon Johnson." *Consequence* was changed into *dignity*, while the compositor was directed to print *Johnson* in "SMALL CAPS," so that the line ran, "a man whose regard reflected dignity even upon JOHNSON."

In the text, as it was published, John Nichols, the editor of the "Gentleman's Magazine," is thus mentioned: "The Editor of that Miscellany in which Johnson wrote for several years seems justly to think that every fragment of so great a man is worthy of being preserved." These lines were inserted instead of the following: "That Mr. Nichols urged him to dispatch is evident from the following sentence in one of his letters to Mrs. Thrale, 'I have finished Prior; so a fig for Mr. Nichols.'" A hit at a Secretary of the Treasury was not allowed to stand. In speaking of "Taxation no Tyranny," Boswell had originally said: "That this pamphlet was written at the desire of those who were then in power I have no doubt; and indeed he owned to me that it had been revised and curtailed by some of them, *he supposed, in particular, Sir Grey Cooper. How humiliating to the great Johnson!*" The words which I have italicised were all struck out. Beauclerk " could not conceive a more humiliating situation than to be clapped on the back by Tom Davies." For Johnson to be corrected by Sir Grey Cooper was perhaps even one step lower in humiliation.

Epithets are occasionally modified, being sometimes strengthened, sometimes softened. Johnson, says Boswell in " The Life " as it now stands, " was treated," at Sir Wolfstan Dixey's, "with what he represented as intolerable harshness." *Intolerable* has been substituted for *brutal*. An attack on Macpherson, and his advocate the Rev. Donald M'Nicol, was made severer in the revise. It had originally stood thus : " At last there came out a scurrilous volume, larger than Johnson's own, filled with *rancorous* abuse, under a name real or fictitious of some low man in an obscure corner of Scotland, though supposed to be the work of *a man better known in both countries.*" For *rancorous* Boswell first substituted *scurrilous*, and then *malignant*, while the words which I have italicised he changed into " another Scotchman, who has found means to make himself well known both in Scotland and England." Macpherson was meant. An attack on Mrs. Thrale he made more severe in the passage where he says that " she frequently practised a coarse mode of flattery." *Coarse* is substituted for *trite*.

To make up for this he modified his mention of her in his note on Mrs. Knowles, the ingenious Quaker lady. He at first wrote, "Dr. Johnson, describing her needle-work in one of his letters to Mrs. Thrale, uses the learned word *sutile;* which Mrs. Thrale not learned has mistaken, and made the phrase injurious by writing *futile.*" *Not learned,* on second thought, he struck out, contented perhaps with having previously let his readers know that Johnson had once said that "her learning was that of a school-boy in one of the lower forms." In quoting one of Johnson's letters to her, he omits some details about health. In a note he had said, "I leave out a few lines, the contents of which are partly too insignificant and partly too indelicate for the publick eye." The "reader" queries, "If not better omitted." Boswell altered it as follows: "I have taken the liberty to leave out a few lines which Mrs. Thrale has printed, but which it appears to me might have been suppressed." The "reader" rejoins, "I think the whole Note would be better omitted and the**** put in a line to shew there was an omission, for it should not be supposed Dr. Johnson wrote anything indelicate to a lady." Boswell yielded so far as to strike out all the note but the first eleven words. The chief indelicacy—and it was a very great one—consisted in Mrs. Piozzi letting the world know that her first husband, after his mind was weakened by a stroke of apoplexy, had been in the habit of eating too much.

In the descriptions of Johnson there are two curious suppressions. "Garrick," Boswell writes, "sometimes used to take him off, squeezing a lemon into a punch-bowl, with uncouth gesticulations, looking round the company and calling out, 'Who's for *poonsh?*'" Boswell added in the margin, "and hands not over-clean. He must have been a stout man, said Garrick, who would have been for it." The "reader" queried, "Should not this be omitted?" The suggestion was taken, and the addition was scored through. In an account of Johnson with which Boswell "was favoured by one of his friends"—most probably Mr. Bowles of Heale—after the words "powerful mind" the following paragraph came in the proof: "He valued himself a good deal on being able to do everything for himself. He visited without a servant when he went to stay at the houses of his friends, and found few or no occasions to employ the servants belonging to the family. He knew how to mend his own stockings, to darn his linen, or to sew a button on his cloaths. 'I am not (he would often say) an [*sic*] helpless man.'" Boswell first corrected "He visited without a servant" by inserting *sometimes*; but in the end he struck out the whole paragraph, writing in the margin, for the compositor's information, "I doubt this, therefore let it go; and thus you may more easily get in a note to Dr. Burney in the next page." Johnson generally took his man with him, the negro Frank Barber, but in his visit to Heale he had left him at home. That he gave but little trouble to servants we know from Mrs. Piozzi, who said that "he required less attendance, sick or well, than ever I saw any human creature." That to some extent he could use a needle is shown by the books which he bound in his old age. The art he had acquired in his father's shop. Nevertheless, when Dempster's sister undertook to teach him to knot, he made no progress.

That after the sheets of "The Life" had been struck off there were two cancels was known by passages in letters written by Boswell to Malone. On January 29, 1791, he wrote: "I am to cancel a leaf of the first volume, having found that though Sir Joshua certainly assured me he had no objection to my mentioning that Johnson wrote a dedication for him he now thinks otherwise." The passage objected to, which came on page 272 of the first volume, was as follows: "*He furnished his friend, Dr Percy, now Bishop of Dromore, with a Dedication to the Countess of Northumberland, which was prefixed to his 'Reliques of ancient English Poetry,' in which he pays compliments to that most illustrious family, in the most courtly style. It should not be wondered at that one who can himself write so well as Dr. Percy should accept of a Dedication from Johnson's pen; for as Sir Joshua Reynolds, who we shall see afterwards accepted of the same kind of assistance, well observed to me, 'Writing a dedication is a knack. It is like writing an advertisement.'*"[1] In this art no man

---

[1] By "advertisement" Reynolds meant a short notice or introduction.

excelled Dr. Johnson. Though the loftiness of his mind prevented him from ever dedicating in his own person, he wrote a great number of Dedications for others. After all the diligence I have bestowed, some of them have escaped my inquiries." The lines italicised have disappeared; while after "Dedications for others" the following was inserted: "Some of these the persons who were favoured with them are unwilling should be mentioned, from a too anxious apprehension, as I think, that they might be suspected of having received larger assistance." It was said that Johnson had assisted Reynolds in his "Discourses." That the Dedication was written by him was, I should have thought, revealed by the style. Who but he could have said that "the regular progress of cultivated life is from necesssaries to accommodations, from accommodations to ornaments"? Nevertheless, in Leslie and Taylor's Life of the great painter we are told that in his Dedication "Reynolds preserved his quiet dignity even in contact with royalty." On this same cancelled page I found a passage which Boswell changed perhaps out of regard to his own dignity. He had written, "I wrote to him frequently in the course of these two years while I was upon my travels, but did not receive a single letter in return." This was altered into, "He did not favour me with a single letter for more than two years."

The second cancel was due to William Gerard Hamilton. On February 25, 1791, Boswell, writing to Malone, said: "That nervous mortal W. G. H. is not satisfied with my report of some particulars *which I wrote down from his own mouth*, and is so much agitated that Courtenay has persuaded me to allow a *new edition* of them, by H. himself to be made at H.'s expense." In this new edition the amended passage is as follows: "Care, however, must be taken to distinguish between Johnson when he 'talked for victory,' and Johnson when he had no desire but to inform and illustrate. '*One of Johnson's principal talents (says an eminent friend of his) was shown in maintaining the wrong side of an argument, and in a splendid perversion of the truth. If you could contrive to have his fair opinion on a subject, and without any bias from personal prejudice, or from a wish to be victorious in argument, it was wisdom itself, not only convincing, but overpowering.*'" The italicised lines, as Boswell first wrote them, had stood thus: "His friend, Mr. Hamilton, when dining at my house one day, expressed this so well that I wrote down his words: 'Johnson's great excellence in maintaining the wrong side of an argument was a splendid perversion. If you could contrive it so as to have his fair opinion upon a subject without any bias from personal prejudice, or from a wish to conquer—it was wisdom, it was justice, it was convincing, it was overpowering.'" The blank in the present text, which comes a few lines lower down, was in the proof filled up with the name of Hamilton. Hamilton, there is good reason to believe, as I have shown in a note at the end of the first volume of my edition of Boswell, when he lost Burke's services in politics, had sought Johnson's aid. Whatever engagement was formed between the two men was kept concealed. The clue to its existence was given by Johnson's Prayer on "engaging in politicks with H——n."

One morning in June, 1784, Boswell " was present at the shocking sight of fifteen men executed before Newgate." Having gratified his miserable curiosity, he naturally went to Bolt Court, hard by, to moralise on free will. " I said to Dr. Johnson I was sure that human life was not machinery—that is to say, a chain of fatality planned and directed by the Supreme Being, as it had in it so much wickedness and misery, so many instances of both, as that by which my mind was now clouded. Were it machinery, it would be better than it is in these respects, though less noble, as not being a system of moral government. He agreed with me, *and added, 'The small-pox can less be accounted for than an execution upon the supposition of machinery; for we are sure it comes without a fault.'*" For the words italicised the following were substituted: " now, as he always did, upon the great question of the liberty of the human will, which has been in all ages perplexed with so much sophistry." In a note for the compositor Boswell added: " I strike out this tho' in my notes, because I do not see the meaning and I may have erred. If you want room *in all ages* may be omitted." Happily, room was found, and *in all ages* stands in the received text.

The insertion of two words in the text led to a note by Croker which provoked an attack by Macaulay in his review of the new edition of the "Life of Johnson." "There is," Macaulay wrote, "a still stranger instance of the editor's talent for finding out difficulties in what is perfectly plain. 'No man,' said Johnson, 'can now be made a bishop for his learning and piety.' 'From this too just observation,' says Boswell, 'there are some eminent exceptions.' Mr. Croker is puzzled by Boswell's very simple and natural language. 'That a general observation should be pronounced *too just* by the very person who admits that it is not universally just is not a little odd.'" *Too just* was inserted in the proof.

One of Croker's conjectures I find confirmed. "Johnson," writes Boswell, "repeated some fine lines on love by Dryden, which I have now forgotten." Croker suggested the verses quoted in the "Lives of the Poets" which begin:—

> "Love various minds does variously inspire;
> It stirs in gentle bosoms [natures] gentle fire,
> Like that of incense on the altar [altars] laid;
> But raging flames tempestuous souls invade."
> *Tyrannic Love*, Act iii. scene 3.

That he was right is shown by the passage in the proof, which originally ran, "He repeated his lines on love ('gentle tempestuous, &c.—')."

In the reports of Johnson's talk a few corrections are made, most of which might be due to previous inaccuracy. That errors were made in copying is shown by a passage in one of his letters, where Boswell, falling into a Scotticism, had at first made him write, "*I will* long to know." *Will* is changed into *shall* in the margin. That Boswell consulted his own note-books we can see by the correction of his report of a saying about Burke. As it stood in the proof Johnson had said: "Yes, Burke is an extraordinary man. His vigour of mind is incessant." The last line Boswell changed into, "His stream of mind is perpetual," adding in the margin, "I restore, I find, the exact words as to Burke." How he gave the wrong words at first is not easy to see, for they were not an isolated saying, but part of a conversation. In like manner he corrects one word in Burke's saying about Croft's imitation of Johnson's style. The line originally stood, "It has all his pomp without his *sense.*" *Sense* was altered into *force*. He now and then inserts *Sir* in the report of the talk, either because it had been omitted by mistake, or—which perhaps is more likely—because it is more the Johnsonian mode. A few of the changes seem to go beyond corrections of the copyist's errors; thus, in the proof, Johnson, speaking of the character of the valetudinarian, had said, "He indulges himself in every way." For the last two words was substituted *the grossest freedoms.*

On Easter Sunday in 1773 Boswell recorded:

"He told me that he had twelve or fourteen times attempted to keep a journal of his life, but never could persevere. He advised me to do it. 'The great thing to be recorded (said he) is the state of your own mind; and you should write down everything that you remember, for you cannot judge at first what is good or bad, and write immediately while the impression is fresh, for it will not be the same a week afterwards.'

"I again solicited him to communicate to me the particulars of his early years. He said, 'You shall have them all for twopence. I hope you shall know a great deal more of me before you write my Life.'" The "reader," it is clear, noticed the different ways in which the talk is recorded in these two paragraphs, and queried against them both, "This almost verbatim?" Boswell replied, "It is much varied, so *stet*." Where he reports the speech in the first person we have Johnson's exact words; where he throws it into the third person we have only an abstract of them. In an earlier passage he had first written, "He recommended to me to keep a journal of my life, fair and undisguised." For *fair and undisguised* he substituted *full and unreserved*. One slight correction is not without interest. In those famous words where Johnson so vigorously gave his opinion of Lady Diana Beauclerk, he had in the proof been made to conclude by saying, "and there's an end *of't*." *Of't* is changed into *on't*.

If Boswell prided himself, and justly prided himself, on "the most perfect authenticity" of his records of conversation, he seems to have thought that, so far as what he had himself said or written, he might now and then indulge in a variation. Thus, in the passage where he reports Johnson's account of his failure to learn knotting, according to the proof, he himself went on to say: "So it will be said, 'Once, for his amusement, he tried knotting,'" &c. This he changed into, "So, sir, it will be related in pompous narrative," &c. Writing to Johnson on February 14, 1777, he said: "You remember poor Goldsmith when he grew important and wished to appear *Doctor Major* could not bear your calling him *Goldy*. Would it not have been somewhat wicked to have named him so in your 'Preface to Shakespeare'?" *Somewhat wicked* he changed into *wrong*. In a letter dated June 9th of the same year, speaking of "what is called 'The *Life* of David Hume,' written by himself, with the letter from Dr. Adam Smith subjoined to it," he continued, "Is not this an age of daring effrontery?" In the margin he substituted *indecency* for *effrontery*, but in the end he struck it out. A few lines lower down he had written, "I agreed with him [Mr. Anderson] that you might knock Hume's and Smith's heads together, and make vain and impudent infidelity exceedingly ridiculous." *Impudent* he thought too offensive even for this offensive passage, for he changed it into *ostentatious*. One change he apparently made to avoid repetition. He had ended one of his letters to his great friend with saying that he was "with affectionate veneration, most affectionately yours, James Boswell." For *affectionately* he substituted *sincerely*. The conclusions of Johnson's letters to him vary, apparently quite by chance, from "Your humble servant" to "Yours most affectionately." A hit at Blair was softened in a passage which now stands, "He praised Blair's sermons : 'Yet,' said he (willing to let us see he was aware that fashionable fame, *however deserved*, is not always the most lasting) 'perhaps they may not be reprinted after seven years ; at least, not after Blair's death.'" The words in italics were added, while the following, which came at the end of the parenthesis, were suppressed, "and to do justice to less showy divines." John Home he had originally described as "the author of Douglas"; this he expanded into "to whom we owe the beautiful and pathetick tragedy of Douglas." Having to mention a Duke of Devonshire, he had merely spoken of him as "the grandfather of the present Duke." This, he saw, was too bald a way of mentioning the owner of Chatsworth ; so "Duke" he changed into "the present representative of that very respectable family." *Respectable*, it must be remembered, in those days "soared fancy's flight" above "a man who kept a gig." George III., when he signed the treaty of peace with the United States, sighed over "the downfall of this once respectable empire." Chesterfield described religion "as too awful and respectable a subject to become a familiar one," and the hour of death as "at least a very respectable one." Adam Smith speaks of "the respectable list of deities into which Alexander the Great had been inserted," and contrasts "the amiable virtues" with "the awful and respectable." Johnson's dead body was called "his respectable remains." A further change was made in this passage about the duke. In the report of what Johnson said of him, after the statement, "He was not a man of superior abilities," came in the proof, "though Basil   would persuade us he was." These words are struck out, Boswell writing in the margin, "This name is too much obliterated for me to read. It begins with K and ends with t—about six or seven letters. I think Kennet." Kennet, no doubt, is the name. Basil Kennet's brother, Bishop Kennet, had preached a funeral sermon on the first duke, who had recommended him to Queen Anne for a deanery. It must have been of the early years of this duke that Basil spoke, for he did not live long enough to see his full manhood. When he was chaplain on a ship of war he cured one of the officers of his habit of interlarding his stories with oaths by parodying him. The words which he inserted in his talk were, however, nothing worse than *bottle*, *pot*, and *glass*. The same story is told of a later divine— Robert Hall, if my memory does not deceive me.

Boswell, in one passage, spoke of "the roughness

which often appeared in Johnson's behaviour." *Often*, when he came to revise the proof, he must have thought too severe, for he changed it into *sometimes*. He hesitated over a word in the humorous account which he gave of Garrick's vanity in his intimacy with Lord Camden. " Why (replied Garrick, with an affected ease, yet as if standing on tiptoe), Lord Camden has this moment left me." For *ease* he substituted *indifference*, then struck it out, but finally adopted it, so that it is *affected indifference* in the text as he published it. In the passage where Boswell tells how Addison and Parnell " were intemperate in the use of wine," he continued, " which Johnson himself in his Lives of *these ingenious, worthy*, and pious men has not forborne to record." For the words in italics he substituted " those celebrated writers." The dissenting minister, Dr. Towers, he had described as " one of the hottest heads of the Revolution Society." *Hottest heads* he changed into *warmest zealots*, perhaps moved by the esteem which he felt for this divine as " a very convivial man." His own Jacobitism he shows in the change which he made in the passage where he speaks of Lord Trimblestown, " in whose family," he originally wrote, " was an ancient Irish peerage, *which was forfeited* in the troubles of the last century." For the words in italics he substituted, " but it suffered by taking the generous side."

He makes now and then an addition to the description which he gives of Johnson. Thus, in his account of one of his great friend's "minute singularities" he had written, "In the intervals of articulating he made various sounds with his mouth, sometimes as if ruminating, or what is called chewing the cud, sometimes giving a half-whistle, sometimes making his tongue play backwards from the roof of his mouth, as if clucking like a hen, and sometimes protruding it against his upper gums in front, as if pronouncing quickly, under his breath, *too, too, too*." Full of life as this description is, how much is it improved by the following addition which Boswell made in the proof: "all this accompanied sometimes with a thoughtful look, but more frequently with a smile." In like manner, the addition of a single word gives liveliness to the famous speech in which Johnson said, "No, sir, claret is the liquor for boys; port for men; but he who aspires to be a hero (smiling) must drink brandy." *Smiling* was added in the revise.

Though I have by no means come to the end of Boswell's corrections, yet I must trespass no further on the patience of my audience. However willing I may be to ride my own hobby to death, I must not either attempt to drag the rest of the world over the whole of the course, or forget that other people have their hobbies too.

THE BOSWELL CENTENARY

A Paper read before the Johnson Club

BY

GEORGE BIRKBECK HILL, D.C.L., LL.D.

Honorary Fellow of Pembroke College, Oxford

JAMES BOSWELL, AFTER SIR THOMAS LAWRENCE.

[To face p. 83

The Boswell Centenary

ONE hundred and thirty-two years ago, in this very month of May, a young Scottish gentleman had the impudence to publish to the world the letters which had passed between himself and a friend. In one of them, written when he was but twenty-one, he said: "I am thinking of the perfect knowledge which I shall acquire of men and manners, of the intimacies which I shall form with the learned and ingenious in every science, and of the many amusing literary anecdotes which I shall record." Never has vanity been better justified. James Boswell did acquire, if not a perfect yet a most curious knowledge of men and manners; he did form not only intimacies but warm friendships with the learned and ingenious, and he not only picked up many amusing literary anecdotes, but he interwove them into a book which is unsurpassed in its kind in any language, and which is read again and again with never-failing pleasure by all classes of men wherever the English tongue is spoken. One of his dreams was not to be realised. "It is not impossible," he wrote, "but that I may catch a little true poetic inspiration, and have my works splendidly printed at Strawberry Hill under the benign influence of the Honourable Horace Walpole." His works were to be handsomely if not splendidly printed, but from poetry he was as wide as the poles asunder. He never got nearer to the Muses than a man can be brought by devotion to the bottle.

In this foolish dream, if he ever really indulged in it, he never indulged long. He was quick in discovering where his true powers lay. Thousands of ambitious youths in every age long for fame: he was one of those few—those happy few—who go the right way to attain it. He saw where the mark lay, and he aimed straight at it. He was a heaven-born biographer, and by a natural instinct he sought the friendship of men whose sayings and doings were worth recording. He was but twenty-two when, full of "a kind of mysterious veneration," he presented himself before that great man who, in his fancy, lived "in a state of solemn elevated abstraction in the immense metropolis of London." The "solemn elevated abstraction" must soon have been dissipated by the port wine and the late hours in which Johnson indulged, but the veneration, though it ceased to be mysterious, was as strong and deep as ever. His hero, in the fierce light that beat upon him in a hundred taverns, remained a hero to the very end. The disciple at once began to record his master's talk. No man had a keener relish for the pleasures of life than Boswell; yet, in these days of his hot youth, in the midst of London, "that heaven upon earth," for which he had "such a gust" as, in Johnson's long and wide experience, had never been felt by any other man, he sat up four nights in one week working at his Journal. It was for no near blaze of triumph, for no "instant reverberation of praise," that he thus laboured. The fame which he longed to secure could not be his till after his hero's death. It was in 1763 that he first met Johnson; not till 1791 was his *Magnum Opus*, as he delighted to call it, given to the world. It was a man of no common character who could plough so deep and sow so diligently for so distant a harvest. When we call to mind all Boswell's weaknesses—weaknesses which ruined his health and brought him to a premature grave—let us not forget how strong he showed himself in his highest and noblest aims.

Meanwhile he was not without a fair measure of fame. His "wise and noble curiosity" led this young man of pleasure to the capital of Corsica, where Paoli was slowly building up a free government. "Boswell had gone," said Johnson, "where, perhaps, no native of Great Britain ever was before." "A man come from Corsica," said Paoli, "will be like a man come from the Antipodes." On his return he published a journal which might well be a model to all travellers. It tells all that is needful to be told, and it is so brief that it can easily be read at a sitting. There is no word-painting in it. That oppressive art had not been invented. Boswell happily knew the exact limits of his literary powers. He found, he confesses, "a great difficulty in describing visible objects," and so he left them undescribed. Johnson pronounced his book "in a very high degree curious and delightful." It moved Gray strangely, though he uttered about it that ridiculous paradox which Macaulay, nearly seventy years later, worked up into a long and splendid passage of extravagant rhetoric. "It proves," said the poet, "that any fool may write a most valuable book by chance, if he will only tell us what he heard and saw with veracity." If Gray had lived out his full share of life, and had read the "Journal of a Tour to the Hebrides" and the "Life of Johnson," he would, we may hope, have admitted that it was no chance that in three books produced such perfect success. He, at all events, who had had the courage to suppress more than one exquisite stanza in his Elegy, knew that the perfection of a work is attained scarcely less by what an author leaves out than by what he puts in. There are, perhaps, no books of the same length as Boswell's two Journals and his "Life of Johnson" in which we wish for so few omissions. Great as was his vanity, he seldom let it mar his writings. When he displays it, and he displays it very often and very openly, he never wearies his reader. Almost always it is connected with the main thread of his narrative. It was with some reason that "in his moments of self-complacency" it seemed to him that his "Life of Johnson" was in one respect like the "Odyssey." "Amidst a thousand entertaining and instructive episodes the hero is never long out of sight ; for they are all in some degree connected with him."

His vanity never offends us, for he never hides it. He never makes use of an artifice to gratify it and to conceal it. It was as well known to himself as it is to his readers. In his "Letter to the People of Scotland" he begs his countrymen to allow him to indulge his egotism and his vanity. "They are," he adds, "the indigenous plants of my mind ; they distinguish it. I may prune their luxuriancy ; but I must not entirely clear it of them ; for then I should be no longer 'as I am,' and perhaps there might be something not so good." Goldsmith, whose failings were almost as great and as ridiculous as Boswell's, like all real humorists, was himself aware of them. In his writings he laughs at them and at himself, sometimes disguising himself under the Vicar of Wakefield and his two sons, sometimes under the Man in Black in "The Citizen of the World." In private life these failings were a constant source of vexation to him, while they often exposed him to the unveiled contempt of his company. He wore them awkwardly ; like his clothes, they never fitted him. Boswell managed his far better. Over Goldsmith's clumsy vanity and his jealous irritability we all grieve; Boswell we would no more have changed than Falstaff. He likes praise, he likes to be talked about, he likes to know great people, and he no more cares to conceal his likings than Sancho Panza cared to conceal his appetite. He is entirely free from hypocrisy.

He is aware of his genius. On one side of his character he knows that he deserves the respect and the gratitude of mankind. His fame he turns to strange account. It is to be a kind of licence—a plenary indulgence to enable him to give full reins to the joyous and animal side of his nature. In the preface to his "Corsica" he writes: "To preserve a uniform dignity among those who see us every day is hardly possible; and to aim at it must put us under the fetters of a perpetual restraint. The author of an approved book may allow his natural disposition an easy play, and yet indulge the pride of superior genius when he considers that by those who know him only as an author he never ceases to be respected."

There was one man, and one man only, before whom his high spirits ever failed him—his genius ever quailed. With Voltaire and Rousseau, Paoli and Hume, Franklin and Johnson, dukes and duchesses, he was at his ease. Even the great Chatham did not overawe him. Before his own father, "I feel myself," he wrote, "like a timid boy, which to *Boswell* (comprehending all that my character does in my own imagination and in that of a wonderful number of mankind) is intolerable." How the old laird came to have such a son we may well wonder. The late Professor Chandler, of Oxford, a sound Johnsonian, as well befitted a member of Johnson's own college, used to maintain that Boswell's strange genius came to him from his great-grandmother, a Dutch lady. If there is little Scottish in his character, still less is there anything Dutch. He was, in truth, as he liked to call himself, "a very universal man," "a citizen of the world." Nevertheless, so peculiarly English is his great work that it has never been translated into a single foreign language.[1] This is due not to Boswell's but to Johnson's nature, "true-born Englishman" that he was.

Wherever Boswell went he rapidly made friends. He was a man of genius, but of that happy genius which is never oppressive. So many-sided was his nature that there were few men with whom he could not live on terms of intimacy. "I lived," he writes, "in habits of friendship with John Wilkes and Samuel Johnson. I could fully relish the excellence of each." Even in his raw student days Adam Smith discovered that he was "happily possessed of a facility of manners."

---

[1] Since I wrote this I have been informed by an anonymous correspondent from St. Petersburg that "a very complete condensation of Boswell's 'Life of Johnson' was published in Russian by a distinguished critic, Drujinine, in 1851 and 1852. It has been republished in his complete works, 1865, and is included in the first 245 close-printed pages of vol. iv."

Hume described him as "very good-humoured, very agreeable, and very mad." "Good-nature," said Burke, "was so natural to him that he had no merit in possessing it; a man might as well assume to himself merit in possessing an excellent constitution." Reynolds esteemed him so highly that he bequeathed to him "£200, to be expended, if he thought proper, in the purchase of a picture at the sale of his paintings, to be kept for his sake." It was for him that Johnson invented the word *clubable*. He once said to him: "Boswell, I think I am easier with you than with almost anybody." "Sir," he said to a friend, "if I were to lose Boswell it would be a limb amputated." "He was," he maintained, "the best travelling companion in the world." He promised "to celebrate his good-humour and perpetual cheerfulness," as shown in their tour to the Hebrides. In truth Boswell had that "most pleasing of all qualities, perpetual gaiety," which Johnson praises so highly in Falstaff.

Happy would it have been for him if his genius had been quickly recognised by the world in which he lived. In that case, satisfied by the fame which he had so fairly earned, he might have refrained from his degrading attempts to rival the Wedderburns and the Dundases by seeking the favour of those whom he called the great. It is melancholy to think that the man who wrote the best biography the world has ever seen day after day danced attendance on a Lord Lonsdale. "The chief glory of every people," says Johnson "arises from its authors." Little of the glory that arises from the immortal "Life" is attributed to the man who wrote it. His great genius, for great it was, has always remained veiled in the cloud of vanities and weaknesses with which it was surrounded. He died just one hundred years ago, on May 19, 1795. No memorial of him exists beyond that imperishable one which he reared to himself. In Edinburgh, the town of his birth, Dundas has his lofty column, and a Duke of Buccleuch his costly statue. The modern Athens has not even marked by an inscription the court in which James Boswell lived. The day, perhaps, will come when his medallion shall be seen in Westminster Abbey, looking down on the graves of Johnson and Garrick, and close to the monument of Goldsmith—three men who live for us in his pages.

DR. JOHNSON AND THE "GENTLEMAN'S MAGAZINE

A Paper read before the Johnson Club
by
ARTHUR WOLLASTON HUTTON

(*First published in the "English Illustrated Magazine."*)

Dr. Johnson and the "Gentleman's Magazine"

ON this auspicious occasion, the twelfth anniversary of the formation of our Club, when there is such a distinguished gathering not only of our noble selves, but also of most welcome guests, I may as well begin by telling the truth, and explain that I have not written the paper I had intended to write. That paper would have been a very remarkable one. Every one knows that there is some obscurity about the contributions of Dr. Johnson to the *Gentleman's Magazine*. I do not mean that the contributions are in themselves obscure, but that there is some uncertainty as to which are his; and this applies especially to what in the *Gentleman's Magazine* is called "poetry." A complete and accurate list even of the prose contributions has never been made out. Boswell gives a list which he admits to be imperfect, and he divides the pieces which it contains into two classes—first, those which are known to be Johnson's because he acknowledged them; and secondly, those which on internal evidence, or as we may say, by means of "the higher criticism," he ascribed to him. In all probability this list does not include several essays and reviews that Johnson really wrote; while, on the other hand, our own immortal ex-Prior, Birkbeck Hill, gives it as his opinion that the equally immortal Boswell was in some cases wrong in his ascription of authorship to the no less immortal Johnson. Indeed, he must have been wrong once or twice, unless we are to suppose that Johnson sometimes wrote bad grammar, which is absurd. Now, the paper which I have not written would have cleared up all doubts on this interesting subject. I had resolved to read with indomitable industry all the papers in the *Gentleman's Magazine* that could by any possibility have been Johnson's; and then, with that fine literary instinct and insight which so few of us possess, while those of us who do possess it are too modest to say so, I should have recognised, and have registered for the benefit of those who come after us, all that was undoubtedly Johnson's; and thenceforward, on the strength of this remarkable paper, I should have deservedly shared immortality with those whom I have named. But alas! these things were not so to be. I set to work with a light heart; but I was baffled by one thing, and by one thing only, and that was the confoundedly small type in which the old *Gentleman's Magazine* was printed. And so it comes to pass that I have now to submit to your charitable judgment a very commonplace paper indeed, dealing, as you will perceive, in but a sorry and ineffectual manner with the mere beggarly elements of my subject.

First, then, it will be well to get a tolerably clear notion of what the *Gentleman's Magazine* was, and of what it was not—I mean, of course, during those fifty years that its existence was contemporaneous with Johnson's life, and especially during those few years, 1738–1748, that he contributed to it. There are well-meaning persons, possibly some of them may even be members of this Club, who imagine that everything written in the eighteenth century must be admirable and precious. I hope to be able to show them that, so far as the *Gentleman's Magazine* is concerned, the great bulk of the literary contributions to it are only precious in the sense of being precious nonsense. How could it have been otherwise, considering what kind of man was Edward Cave, the editor with whom Johnson had to do?

Born at Rugby in 1691, the son of a cobbler, he had none the less the right of admittance to Rugby School; but he was very shortly expelled from it for robbing the hen-roost of the Head Master's wife. He then became clerk to a Collector of Excise; and it may be conjectured that it was from Cave that Johnson first learnt to regard a Commissioner of Excise as "one of the lowest of all human beings," and excise itself as "a hateful tax levied ... by wretches hired by those to whom excise is paid." A little later he was apprenticed to a printer; then was employed in the Post Office; and soon he obtained the post, that of " Clerk of the Franks" in the Houses of Parliament, which, by bringing him into contact with statesmen and politicians, laid the foundation of his subsequent career. He picked up news of a kind that was in those days reckoned confidential, and sent it to the country papers. Very soon he was imprisoned for such a breach of privilege; and, though he was purged of this offence by a fine, his thirst for knowledge was so insatiable that he was a little later dismissed from his post on the charge of opening letters that had been entrusted to him.

Thus admirably trained for the post of magazine editor, he bought, in 1731, a small printing office in St. John's Gate, Clerkenwell, and began business under the name of " R. Newton, printer "; at the same time starting the *Gentleman's Magazine,* as "edited by Sylvanus Urban, of Aldermanbury, Gent." Literary power he himself had none; but, through some sort of instinct, he was none the less a capable editor. His troubles with the Legislature did not cease when he had left Westminster for Clerkenwell. There was " high indignation" in the Commons when, in 1738, he published a Royal reply to an Address before it had been reported to the Speaker; and in

ST. JOHN'S GATE, CLERKENWELL.

(Drawn by S. J. Hodson, Brother of the Johnson Club.)

[To face p. 99.

THE "GENTLEMAN'S MAGAZINE"

1747 he was reprimanded by the Lords, on his knees, for having printed an account of the trial of Lord Lovat. Evidently he was an enterprising and up-to-date editor; and it may be interesting also to record that, although he never took any exercise beyond an occasional game of battledore and shuttlecock in a room over St. John's Gate, and was for a long time a vegetarian, and, during all the years that Johnson knew him never drank anything but milk and water, he was none the less a big, strong man. Nor was his character without attractive features. In days when we are all sorely tempted to invent for ourselves imposing coats-of-arms, and to imagine that we are descended from a long and illustrious ancestry, it is pleasant to remember that in his later years the editor of the *Gentleman's Magazine* liked nothing so well as to be called "Old Cave, the cobbler"; and that, when his growing wealth warranted him in purchasing an ancient coach and a still more ancient pair of horses, he was content to have painted on the coach-panel, in place of a fictitious coat-of-arms, a representation of St. John's Gate, in which for over twenty years he worked as printer and editor. Such was the man with whom Johnson, so far as concerns his connection with the *Gentleman's Magazine*, had to deal. On January 10, 1754, he died, "gently pressing Johnson's hand."

Next, as to the magazine itself. It was the first publication ever so styled, and the word seems to have been frankly and accurately used in its proper sense of "receptacle." I have my eye now on those well-meaning persons already referred to, who imagine that because the *Gentleman's Magazine* contains essays written in the eighteenth century, it is therefore a magazine containing priceless literature. I am bold enough to maintain that it is nothing of the sort. So far as literature, in the strict sense, is concerned, the *Gentleman's Magazine* is a wilderness of deservedly forgotten rubbish. Indeed, in its early days it hardly pretended to high literary merit. Its first number had the sub-title of, *or Traders' Monthly Intelligencer;* and though this was dropped in the second number, and *Historical Chronicle* substituted, it still prided itself more on the voluminousness of its contents than on their quality. "Containing more than any other book," or, a little later, "containing more in quantity and greater variety than any book of the kind and price"—such was its boast. Nor did it even claim originality for its contents; they were "collected chiefly from the public papers"; and, if it promised literature at all, it was to be the work of fifth-rate scribblers, whose souls could rise no higher than to such grammar-school pseudonyms as "Mr. Bavius," "Mr. Mævius," "Mr. Spondee," "Mr. Dactyl," "Mr. Quidnunc," "Mr. Conundrum," "Mr. Orthodoxo," who treated of theology, and "Dr. Quibus," who treated of medicine. Such was the abysmally low literary level of the magazine to which Johnson, in his twenty-fifth

THE "GENTLEMAN'S MAGAZINE"

year, first proposed to contribute, poverty and nothing else thereunto urging him. I am far from denying that in other aspects it was a most useful and even entertaining publication. Were it not for its excruciatingly small type, a volume of the old *Gentleman's Magazine* would often be found vastly more instructive and amusing than a volume of an up-to-date magazine of to-day. I am speaking only of the quality of its literature and of its poetry—oh, such poetry!—for it was as a literary man that our Johnson was forced by fate to seek to become a contributor to the magazine in the fourth year of its existence.

We have Johnson's letter to Cave, written in 1734, and first published in 1785, after Johnson's death. It is an interesting example of the way in which you should *not* approach an editor if you wish him to accept your contribution—

"SIR,—As you appear no less sensible than your readers of the defects of your poetical article, you will not be displeased if, in order to the improvement of it, I communicate to you the sentiments of a person who will undertake, on reasonable terms, sometimes to fill a column. His opinion is that the publick would not give you a bad reception, if, besides the current wit of the month, which a critical examination would generally reduce to a narrow compass, you admitted not only poems, inscriptions, etc., never printed before [I like that description of one's own poetical effusions—

" poems never printed before "], which he will sometimes supply you with, but likewise short literary dissertations in Latin or English, critical remarks on authors, ancient or modern, forgotten poems that deserve revival, or loose pieces, like Floyer's, worth preserving. [Floyer's "loose piece" was an essay on the advantage of occasionally taking a bath; and it attracted considerable attention from the novelty of the idea.] By this method your literary article, for so it might be called, will, he thinks, be better recommended to the publick than by low jests, awkward buffoonery, or the dull scurrilities of either party. If such a correspondence will be agreeable to you, be pleased to inform me in two posts what the conditions are on which you shall expect it. Your late offer gives me no reason to distrust your generosity. [It was an offer of £50 for the best poem on "Life, Death, Judgment, Heaven, and Hell"—rather a comprehensive subject.] If you engage in any literary projects besides this paper, I have other designs to impart, if I could be secure from having others reap the advantage of what I should hint. Your letter, by being directed to S. Smith, to be left at the Castle [doubtless a tavern] in Birmingham, Warwickshire, will reach your humble servant."

The letter shows much ability and shrewdness; but it was far too frank for its purpose. Cave did indeed reply, but he declined Johnson's offer.

THE "GENTLEMAN'S MAGAZINE"

The year following (1735) Johnson married Mrs. Porter; and in 1736 he contrived to get a brief composition of his own inserted in the magazine by a method which is open to the humblest of us—namely, by advertising. "At Edial [now spelt Edgehill] near Lichfield in Staffordshire, young gentlemen are boarded and taught the Latin and Greek languages by Samuel Johnson." It is interesting to note, with reference to this advertisement, as illustrating what I said about the miscellaneous and not purely literary class in which the magazine circulated, that the only other advertisement in this number, besides Johnson's, and five of new books, is one from a Dublin plasterer for his runaway apprentice, whom he describes as about 5 feet 8 high, pale face, long nose, large, full eye, *and very much opinionated in the way of his trade*. His master hopes no person whatever will employ the said Keating after this notice given." In the purely literary periodicals of the eighteenth century one would no more look for an advertisement for a runaway plasterer than one would look for it now in the *Athenæum* or the *Spectator*.

If only three pupils resulted from Johnson's advertisement, one of them, at any rate, was David Garrick; but the school project soon proved a failure; and Johnson came up to London, accompanied by Garrick, he, as he used to say afterwards, with twopence-halfpenny in his pocket, and his companion with three-halfpence. Passing through London he saw St.

John's Gate, Clerkenwell, and "beheld it with reverence," as the shrine of the *Gentleman's Magazine;* and from Greenwich he again wrote to Cave, this time with a fresh proposal, but no more success. In March, 1738, however, a new light broke upon him, and he perceived that a true way to an editor's heart is neither learning nor ability, nor any nonsense of that kind, but simply flattery. So he addressed to Cave a Latin ode of six stanzas, beginning—

> "*Urbane, nullis fesse laboribus,
> Urbane, nullis victe calumniis,*"

and stuffed full of similar compliments, and the editor was caught. The ode was, of course, accepted and printed; and thenceforward, Boswell tells us, "Johnson was enlisted by Mr. Cave as a regular coadjutor in his magazine, by which he probably obtained a tolerable livelihood." A tolerable livelihood! Well, we know that he received five guineas for his translation of Lobo's "Voyage to Abyssinia"; we know that in two years he was paid nearly fifty pounds for work done at his abortive translation of Father Paul's "History of the Council of Trent"; and we also know that Johnson said he could live on thirty pounds a year "without being contemptible." But we must not forget that in 1739, a year after he had secured admission to the *Gentleman's Magazine,* he tried to obtain the masterhip of a school at Appleby, because, as he said, he was "being starved to death by translating for booksellers, which had been his only subsistence for some time past," words implying that Cave paid him little or nothing for his contributions to the magazine. And we may recall that, after Cave's death, though he always spoke of him with affection, yet he said he was "a penurious paymaster; he would contract for lines by the hundred, and expect the long hundred."

It was in strange company that Johnson found himself when he had at last obtained admission to the columns of the *Gentleman's Magazine*. His first contribution was a sketch of the life of Father Paul, intended to call attention to his projected translation of the "History of the Council of Trent"—a grave if not a dull article. It occupied about the middle of the number, and it was preceded by the "Parliamentary Debates," then written by Guthrie; "Observations on Lapland," "Dr. Boerhaave's Receipt for an Ulcer in the Bowels"; an article entitled "What is Love?" and then "A Modest Epitaph." Following it we have a discussion "Whether Conjugal Happiness decreasing after Marriage is not a Discouragement to Matrimony"; then "French Fashions Exploded: Modern Travellers recommended to Old Soho as the proper Place to learn the French Air and Language"; and other rubbish of the same kind.

The next issue, for June 1739, contains, as Johnson's contribution, an elaborate analysis, extending to seven columns, and "to be continued," of "Four Sermons by the Rev. Joseph Trapp, D.D., on the Nature, Folly, Sin, and Danger of being Righteous Overmuch"—a subject on which our chaplain would probably think it unnecessary to enlarge before the present company; and, after that, the editor returns, with obvious delight, to a medical subject. He had, it would appear, induced a Mrs. Stephens to make "a full discovery" of the ingredients in her wonderful powder, decoction, and pills.

Johnson's "Parliamentary Debates" were, as is well known, first contributed to the columns of the magazine; and they have been reprinted among his works; but it may be doubted whether it was quite fair to his reputation that this should have been done. His saying is familiar, that in these reports he "took care that the Whig dogs should not have the best of it"; but it is not, perhaps, so generally known that he was never himself present at any of the debates which he nevertheless reported. Occasionally a member of Parliament would send privately to the editor in writing what he had said or intended to say in the House; but, as Johnson admitted, the reports were often "the mere coinage of his own imagination." And in his later years he confessed that these Debates were "the only parts of his writings which gave him any compunction. At the time he wrote them he had no conception he was imposing upon the world, though they were frequently written from very slender materials, and often from none at all."

Stuff of this kind he wrote with extraordinary velocity; indeed, this seems to have been true of all his contributions to the *Gentleman's Magazine*. Three columns in an hour was no uncommon effort for him; and he only surpassed himself when he wrote the "Life of Savage," producing then as many as forty-eight octavo pages in the course of one day, a day, however, which "included part of the night." A sentence or two from Johnson's anonymous announcement in the magazine that he had this work in hand is not without interest, as displaying some vigour in self-assertion: "A Life of the unfortunate and ingenious Mr. Savage will speedily be published by a person who was favoured with his confidence. Others may have the same design; but as it is not creditable that they can obtain the same materials, it must be expected that they will supply from invention the want of intelligence." And in the preface which Johnson wrote to the volume for 1745 there are some phrases which have a singularly up-to-date ring. He claims that the rivalry of other magazines had resulted only in his own editor's "researches into writers of a higher class and subjects of universal utility"; and he specifies "the new and surprising accounts of electricity, the caution against burying alive . . . seasonable rules for preserving cattle from the present distemper . . . articles, many of them investigated from foreign authors [I like that word "investigated," used in the sense of "cribbed"], with similar instances of our diligence or happy correspondence not to be found in any other collection." Such things, he maintains, "still give this magazine the preference, and render it a fund of profit and entertainment to the learned, ingenious, and public-spirited."

And now a word as to Johnson's poetry in the *Gentleman's Magazine*. According to Boswell, these contributions were "very numerous"; and, if that be so, it is certain that numbers of them have never been identified, and (may I add) it is to be hoped they never will be. Johnson, although a first-rate critic of poetry, was hardly himself a first-rate poet; though, indeed, we have learnt, on the excellent authority of our brother Birrell, that Tennyson was a warm admirer of some of his longer poems, such as "London." But if it be the case that even his best efforts in this department of literature find but few readers now, it would be unfair to his memory to gather up, and to label as his, fragments which he himself frankly despised, and wrote only with a view to bread-and-cheese. We are all familiar with the metrical rubbish which every educated person in the eighteenth century thought it his or her duty to furnish on demand for young ladies' albums and other such receptacles. Many of them could do it, too, with as much ease and regularity as a hen lays eggs. You have endless odes "To Venus" or "To Cupid." You have also an "Ode to a Fan returned to Miss ———, after having been Broken in a Dance"; or, again, "Verses on the Instability of Human Perfections," and so forth and so forth. It is all correct enough in form, but it is all sadly lacking in vigour and poetic inspiration. Johnson easily wrote this kind of thing; but, I repeat, he also despised it. To Cave, who had desired for the magazine some "Verses to Lady Firebrace," he replied: "They may be had when you please, for you know that such a subject neither deserves much thought nor requires it." Certainly his familiarity with Latin and Greek set him in this matter a head and shoulders above his contemporaries. When, for example, he was minded to address some verses to "the excellent Miss Carter"—a "new woman" of those days—it took the form of a Greek epigram "To Eliza," with which the lady was doubtless mightily pleased. But it was his fatal facility in such compositions, and the pressure of poverty that daily cried aloud to him to use his gift, that made him thus write, rather than the presence of the divine fire of poetry within his soul. Indeed, his definition of poetry in his Dictionary as "metrical composition" shows that he had an eye more to an accident of its form than to that which is essential to its very being; and when one day Boswell asked him, "Then, Sir, what is poetry?" he replied with unusual evasiveness, "Why, Sir, it is much easier to say what it is not." Well, if any one cares to wade through the columns and columns of "poetry" in the *Gentleman's Magazine*, he will, I think, gain a very clear conception of what it is not.

I will give, however, one not unpleasing example of this facility of Johnson's. Garrick had recited to him a metrical epitaph, by a certain Dr. Wilkes, on Claudy Philips, a poor musician—

> "Exalted soul, whose harmony could please
> The love-sick virgin and the gouty ease;
> Could jarring discord, like Amphion, move
> To beauteous order and harmonious love,
> Rest here in peace till angels bid thee rise,
> And meet thy blessed Saviour in the skies."

This last couplet sounds like a commonplace from other epitaphs. Anyhow, we are told that Johnson "shook his head at these funereal lines," and said to Garrick, 'I think, Davy, I can make a better.'" Then, stirring about his tea for a little while in a state of meditation, he almost extempore produced the following verses—

> "Philips, whose touch harmonious could remove
> The pangs of guilty power or hapless love,
> Rest here, distressed by poverty no more,
> Here find that calm thou gav'st so oft before;
> Sleep undisturbed within this peaceful shrine,
> Till angels wake thee with a note like thine."

Johnson is certainly to be preferred to Wilkes; and it is interesting to learn, on his own authority, that angels play the fiddle, an instrument which he could not endure. But now hear the plain prose facts, as stated in the man's own actual epitaph, still to be seen in Wolverhampton Church; and judge whether it was worth while to turn into second-rate poetry what had already been expressed in first-rate prose—

> *Near this place lies*
> CHARLES CLAUDIUS PHILIPS,
> *whose absolute contempt of riches
> and inimitable performances upon the violin
> made him the admiration of all that knew him.
> He was born in Wales;
> made the tour of Europe;
> and, after the experience of both kinds of fortune,
> Died in 1732.*

There is a touch of genius in that collocation of the "absolute contempt of riches" with "inimitable performances upon the violin," which surpasses anything you can find in all the poetry in the *Gentleman's Magazine*.

I am coming to an end. After 1745 Johnson seldom wrote anything for Cave. It was in that year that he contemplated an edition of Shakespeare; but the proposal came to nothing. In 1747 he put forth his plan for a "Dictionary of the English Language"; but of this epoch-making project no notice whatever appeared in the columns of the *Gentleman's Magazine*. It is conjectured that at this date Cave and Johnson were not on good terms. At any rate, in 1748, when he began to work at the Dictionary, he sent Cave his last contribution. He had now, I take it, escaped from what may be described from one point of view as the prison-house, or from another as the playground of his genius, into the liberty of a purer air; and his work was no longer subject to the revision, perhaps even to the rejection, of a well-meaning but obviously Philistine editor. Johnson, as we know and revere him, is not the Johnson who contributed to the *Gentleman's Magazine* because he wanted the wherewithal to keep body and soul together, but the emancipated Johnson of the Dictionary, the "Rambler," the "Idler," and the rest. In some sense, indeed, the magazine had given him a start; and after his death it overwhelmed his memory with praises. "On December 13, a little before seven in the evening," so we read in the obituary column of the number for December, 1784, "without a pang, though long before oppressed with a complication of dreadful maladies, [died] the great and good Dr. Samuel Johnson, the pride of English literature and of human nature"; with much more in exaggerated though honest laudation. There may be found also in this same number a biographical sketch of him, extending over more than twenty-five columns, a copy of his will and its codicil, an account of his post-mortem, and of the funeral in Westminster Abbey of so much of his remains as the doctors had not appropriated. And in the number for January, 1785, many of his letters were printed.

But the last composition of Johnson's that was printed in the magazine during his lifetime was a considerable extract from his Preface to the Dictionary, which appeared when that great work was reviewed on its publication, in April, 1755. The review itself is poor enough : it is hardly more than a dry analysis of the scope of the Dictionary, together with a few somewhat obvious remarks upon it. But the writer had felt the power and the charm of Johnson's Preface, and he quoted largely from it.

Perhaps it would have been in accordance with the fitness of things had Cave lived a few months longer, so as to witness and to ponder over this great achievement of his once rejected contributor. Yet it may have been best as it was. Johnson, at any rate, though never adequately appreciated by Cave, had no desire to gain a personal victory over him. He was by nature too generous not to forget old sores, when, after much struggling, he had, at the age of five-and-forty, secured lasting fame.

DR. JOHNSON'S LIBRARY

A Paper read before the Johnson Club

BY

ARTHUR WOLLASTON HUTTON, M.A.

At Oxford, June 11, 1892

DR. JOHNSON IN HIS TRAVELLING DRESS.
(See note in List of Illustrations.)

[To face p. 117.

Dr. Johnson's Library

WHEN first invited to read a paper at this most important and interesting meeting of our society, I asked the venerable official to whom the Johnson Club owes so much—not the least of our debts being that he has had reprinted and is about to distribute to us to-day a facsimile of the sale-catalogue of Dr. Johnson's library—I, as being a novice among you, asked him how long my paper ought to be; and he replied promptly, "Cut it short, a quarter of an hour at the outside; less if possible." This admirable reply, so characteristic of the Scribe's business-like habits, put me into rather an awkward position, for I had been calculating that it would take me full twenty minutes to make an adequate apology for my reading a paper at all. The brethren are so modest that they always begin by pointing out that it would have been far better if some one else had been selected, that the occasion demanded the services of some more distinguished brother, and so on, and so on; and I had quite made up my mind that, however much I might fail in other matters, I would be second to none in modesty; but this rigid rule has thwarted me, and I must proceed at once to business, and ask the brethren and our distinguished guests to be content with matter, which, though it will probably be less valuable than this suppressed apology, will, at any rate, be more directly connected with our profession as Johnsonians.

Yet I cannot begin without some reference to the place where we are assembled; to this much-loved University, which Johnson, as an undergraduate, did something to discredit—though in latter years he became one of its greatest glories—to this ancient seat of learning; so-called, it was understood in my day, because here the Middle Ages were, twenty years ago, still reckoned well up to date, while learning had here sat down to enjoy eternal repose. All this doubtless is changed now; yet our kindly mother is not so unlike her old self, but that I, at any rate, can thankfully recall some seven happy, wasted years spent beneath her sheltering wing.

To business, however, now, without further preface. I am supposed to be going to read a paper on Dr. Johnson's library; but in point of fact I have to deal with that library only after it had ceased to be Dr. Johnson's, for my text-book is its sale-catalogue. My subject is thus a melancholy one, and I trust the brethren will meet me half way in a duly melancholy spirit, for I do not want to go all the way myself. This sale-catalogue is rather a rarity. There is no copy of it in the British Museum, but there is one in the Bodleian; so that I may assume that its contents are familiar to all Oxford residents. A copy of it came by chance into the hands of our brother Tregaskis; and he, with commendable loyalty to the Club, regarded it as a find, not for his own benefit, but for the benefit of us all; and he brought it to the Scribe, who, as I have said, had it reprinted in facsimile, and has given a copy of the reprint to every one present here to-night. All this is praiseworthy and admirable; but when we turn to the catalogue itself, it is but a very sorry production, sadly unworthy of the occasion that called it into existence. That the cataloguer of the Harleian Library should have had his own books thus catalogued is a melancholy thought, and makes one reflect on what may happen to any of us when we are gathered to our cataloguers and biographers. The first Christie, the auctioneer who is responsible for this catalogue, and who sold the books in Pall Mall in February, 1785, had resigned a commission in the navy in order to become an auctioneer. It is a pity he did not remain in the navy. Hardly an entry in the catalogue is free from mistakes; hardly any book is adequately described, so as to place the edition beyond doubt; some of the entries are so incomplete that the book is unrecognisable; while every lot

contains a number of books that are not named at all.
So that, although there are only 662 lots, I have found,
by adding up the numbers in each, that 3,000 volumes
were sold in the four days, not counting bundles of
pamphlets, such as lots 631 and 632, which may have
included scarce and very valuable matter. The sale
too was sadly unproductive. The whole amount
realised was £242 9s., being at an average of about
nineteen pence a volume, a truly lamentable result,
considering that the library included many valuable
editions of the classics printed in the sixteenth century,
and the first folio edition of Shakespeare, which, if in
good condition, as it probably was not, ought to have
fetched more than what the whole library went for.
So much for a general survey of this deplorable catalogue and this deplorable sale. If we turn now to
sundry details, with the view of estimating Dr. Johnson's literary tastes by the contents of his library, we
find, no doubt, an endless fund of entertainment, but
we are precluded from drawing any definite conclusion
by the fact that, while only about one-fifth of the
books sold are named, Johnson, shortly before his
death, gave away a number of books to his friends,
though he somehow forgot to give any to poor Boswell.
It is, however, natural to suppose that he would at
such a time give away some of his favourites, though
he was not an advocate of giving books away under
ordinary circumstances. If an author wanted his books
to be read, he should, Johnson thought, sell them at a

low price, but not give them; for books given are not valued and are not read. He did, however, once give away a book himself, under circumstances that might well move his rugged soul. The anecdote is to be found both in Boswell's "Life," and in that new and admirable collection of Johnson's letters, by editing which our beloved and honoured Prior has placed us all under a fresh obligation to him. It was during the Scotch tour, and it was at a place called Anoch or Enoch in Glenmoriston, nine miles from Fort Augustus, a collection of hovels, among which the inn was distinguished by having a chimney. Here the doctor had to put up for the night, and gave vent to some excusable spleen. But "in the afternoon," he says, "tea was made by a very decent girl in a printed linen; she engaged me so much that I made her a present of Cocker's arithmetic." Perhaps he suspected that she was of a literary turn, as even her linen was printed. At a later date, however, he explained how he "happened to have about him" such a remarkable book: "Why, sir, if you are to have but one book with you upon a journey, let it be a book of science." He added about the "very decent girl," "I should not be pleased to think that she forgets me"; and let us hope she did not. He did not, however, always keep to science when he was travelling; for in the year 1763, when going down to Harwich by the stage coach, in which his companions, besides Boswell, were "a fat elderly gentlewoman and a young Dutchman," "he had in his pocket 'Pomponius Mela de Situ Orbis,' in which he read occasionally, and seemed very intent upon ancient geography." But, returning to our catalogue and taking it for what it is worth, it is noticeable how Johnson rose superior to the mere curious book-collector. Opportunities he must have had in abundance for placing in his shelves specimens of early printing; yet in his library it appears there was only one fifteenth-century printed book, and that is lot 295, "Boethius on the Consolation of Philosophy," one of the least rare among the *incunabula*, as some five-and-twenty editions of it were printed before the year 1500. Of sixteenth-century books there are fifty-six in all, including Barclay's "Ship of Fools"—not the first edition, but that printed in 1570—a book, "the very mention of which excites the enthusiasm of the true bibliomaniac." Johnson refers to it in a letter to Thomas Warton, and offers to procure a copy for him from Dodsley, if he cannot find it for himself. The brethren will pardon me if I quote some quaint satirical lines from this book, spoken by the first fool in the ship, "The Ignorant Bookworm," but whom I would rather describe as "The Incompleat Librarian." One can imagine Johnson reading them with a grim but not unkindly smile:—

> "Lo, in likewise of bookes I have store,
> But few I reade and fewer understande;
> I folowe not their doctrine nor their lore,
> It is enough to bear a book in hande:

DR. JOHNSON'S LIBRARY

It were too much to be in such a lande
For to be bound to look within the booke :
I am content on the faire covering to look.
Still am I busy, books assembling,
For to have plentie, it is a pleasant thing,
In my conceit to have them aye at hand ;
But what they mean do I not understande.
But yet I have them in great reverence
And honour, saving them from filth and ordure,
By often brushing and much diligence :
Full goodly bound in pleasant coverture
Of damas, satin, orels of velvet pure :
I keep them sure, fearing lest they should be lost,
For in them is the cunning wherein I me boast.
But if it fortune that any learned man
Within my house fall to disputation,
I drawe the curtains to shewe my books then,
That they of my cunning should make probation :
I love not to fall in altercation :
And while the common my bookes I turn and winde,
For all is in them, and nothing in my minde."

What could be a greater contrast to Dr. Johnson in his library? While here at Oxford an old gentleman said to him, "Young man, ply your book diligently now, and acquire a stock of knowledge ; for when years come upon you, you will find that poring upon books will be but an irksome task." And, despite a desultory temperament, which has, perhaps, been mistaken for indolence, Johnson was faithful to this advice. It is true that he preferred conversation to reading ; yet he maintained that knowledge could never be properly acquired by conversation. "The foundation must be laid by reading ; in conversation you never get a system." It is true that he did not read books through to the end, and doubted whether any one ever did so; but this was rather due to the quickness of his literary insight, and to that weariness which overcomes us all when we see what an author is driving at, and wish him to say so and have done with it. To Mrs. Thrale he wrote that "Don Quixote," "Robinson Crusoe," and the "Pilgrim's Progress," are the only books that readers ever wished were longer; and modern taste would hardly even make these exceptions. Yet (to quote our Prior's never-sufficiently-to-be-praised index to Boswell) he read "rapidly," "ravenously," "like a Turk"—rather an ambiguous phrase in this connection—and "sometimes amused himself with very slight reading"; but the bulk of his reading was of a very serious kind; and when one looks through the long list of Greek and Latin authors in his library—and were in his mind as well as in his bookshelves—and notices many names quite unfamiliar to us now, we can give credence to the statement that classical scholarship, as a living thing, hardly survived the eighteenth century.

But Johnson's library was far from being exclusively classical; it was well stocked with books illustrating his taste for controversial theology, and it showed also an interest in law and in medicine; while there were a number of such books as Selden's "Titles of Honour," "which no gentleman's library should be without." There was little, however, to show that he cared for what he would have called "natural philosophy," and we should call physical science; the only noticeable exception being "Brown's Vulgar Errors," a work by the author of "Religio Medici," which really bears the more imposing title of "Pseudodoxia Epidemica." Even in the last century, however, this was an old-world book of science, for it takes pains to explode, on scientific grounds, such fables as those of the phœnix. In other departments there are sundry books which may cause the brethren to raise their eyebrows in astonishment that such should have been found on Dr. Johnson's shelves. There is an airiness about lot 81, "Mercurialis de Arte Gymnastica," which we do not readily associate with the ponderous doctor; and what should he want with lot 85, "Astruc de Morbis Veneris"? or how could he find pleasure in reading lot 121, "Mudge on the Small-pox"? Perhaps he did not read the book, for probably he did not buy it, the author, a surgeon who "practised with great reputation at Plymouth," having asked the doctor to be godfather to his child, and doubtless giving him this lively book by way of a fee. His father too, the Rev. Zachariah Mudge, Prebendary of Exeter, who died in 1769, had been held in high esteem by Johnson, who said of him that "though studious he was popular, though argumentative he was modest, though inflexible he was candid, and though metaphysical yet orthodox." Johnson's criticism on this excellent man's sermons (lot 26) may also be of service to the brethren; for, though I fear they seldom hear sermons, there are doubtless several who write for the market. "Mudge's sermons," he said to Sir Joshua Reynolds, "are good but not practical. He grasps more sense than he can hold; he takes more corn than he can make into meal; he opens a wide prospect, but it is so distant it is indistinct. I love Blair's sermons. Though the dog is a Scotchman and a Presbyterian and everything he should not be, I was the first to praise them; such was my candour." There is, however, one medical work in Johnson's library, one that he valued highly and recommended to Boswell, the title of which cannot be read without a pathetic interest, when we recall the affliction that made a martyrdom of much of Johnson's life: it is lot 124, Cheyne's "English Malady." The author is described as "a very religious man who wrote 'Observations on the Gout,'" and the sub-title of the book that Johnson had, and read, we know, with hopes alternating with despair, is "a Treatise of nervous diseases of all kinds, as spleens, vapours, lowness of spirits, hypochondriacal and hysterical distempers;" and it is one, I take it, that, in the present race for wealth and pre-eminence, "no gentleman should be without." The author was in his profession far in advance of his age; for he taught that the physician's art lay rather in prescribing diet than drugs.

Only one other book will I mention in this catalogue, which tempts one to make reflections in so many directions, and that is lot 210, Wood's "Athenæ Oxonienses." Every action of Johnson's life is known to our Prior, and so I will ask him to tell us later in the evening whether this is the copy that in 1755 Johnson asked Dr. Bird to lend him for a few days.

Johnson in truth lived amidst books and bookmen, so that we have a veritable embarrassment of riches when we seek to learn the principles on which his library was selected. But there is a letter, written in 1768, to be found in that excellent edition of the "Letters" to which I have already referred, where Johnson, with unusual care, gives his views on book-collecting. He was careful because he was writing to the King's librarian at Windsor, and it was clearly in his mind that the letter would come under the King's eye, and that in consequence he would sooner or later "hear of something to his advantage," which alas! he never did. The letter was written to Frederick, afterwards Sir Frederick Barnard—for I may explain that even librarians are not always exempt from that honour which we more commonly associate with extra-sophistical barristers, with smooth-tongued medicine-men, with finance-mongering lord mayors, or with gouty and inefficient generals—who was about to travel on the Continent—"a part of the world," Johnson remarks, "divided between bigotry and atheism," to purchase books for the King. It is full of sensible advice. He points out, what is to the purpose in days when the first-edition craze is rampant, that while the first edition may be the most curious, the last will be the most useful; and he is a little satirical about books, "the mere rarity of which makes the value," while others "are prized at a high rate by a wantonness rather than by use." The whole letter is worth reading.

But I have reached the limits set me by the Scribe, and I will wind up with all decent speed. I am glad, however, to be able to use an occasion so memorable as this meeting will always be in the annals of our Club—memorable, because we have still in the Prior's chair the most distinguished Johnsonian scholar of this and perhaps of any day—memorable, because of our place of meeting, full of associations with Johnson's earlier life—memorable, because of an unusually large company of distinguished guests who have honoured us with their company this evening—and memorable not the least on account of the courtesy and hospitality shown to us at this time by Dr. Johnson's own college —I am glad to be able to use such an occasion to make a recantation—and recantations are rather in my line. When some years since I was first honoured by being invited as a guest to a supper of this Club, of which now I am proud to be the youngest brother, I was unwise enough to say that I was not an admirer of the great Johnson, not at any rate in all respects. I will now apologise and explain. Shortly before that meeting I happened to be discussing Dr. Johnson's position in the progress of thought with Mr. Frederic

DR. JOHNSON'S LIBRARY

Harrison; and he used of him an expression which I now perceive was flat blasphemy as ever was committed; he called him "the prince of Philistines." I was rather taken with the phrase at the time, and thought it a not inapt description of a man who, for one thing, had no music in his soul—a point on which I need not insist beyond recalling the delightful paper on the subject read at our last meeting—and who was also so devoid of political insight that, though he actually lived up to within five years of the great era of revolution, he had no presentiment whatever of its approach. What forcible language would he not have used had he been told of the coming of Auguste Comte and of the Positivist calendar! But I have since come to see that, while it is easy for a German or an Englishman who has got a little French polish upon him, to talk airily and contemptuously about "Philistines," this is not a true criticism of life. In the rugged greatness of Johnson's noble character, which I could wish his library catalogue reflected more adequately, but which is clearly recognisable in his letters and in Boswell's immortal "Life," I can now see a true humanity, in comparison with which political insight becomes a trivial detail; and, though I am sorry about the music and cannot altogether excuse it, I anticipate that, as years go on, and I become more familiar with Johnson's fidelity to great principles, with his tender and affectionate side as well as with his sturdy common-sense, with his candour, his shrewdness, and his appreciation of the vastly great importance of the part played in life by friendship and a companionable spirit, I may be able to subscribe myself, as Malone did, and as another has done, whose name is always to be held in honour in Oxford, the present Master of Balliol [1]—*Johnsonianissimus.*

[1] Benjamin Jowett.

SOME JOHNSON CHARACTERISTICS

A PAPER READ BEFORE THE JOHNSON CLUB

BY

By H. W. MASSINGHAM

TEA. CARICATURE, AFTER A DESIGN BY SAMUEL COLLINGS.

Some Johnson Characteristics.[1]

I PROPOSE to say a word about Johnson's characteristics and writings rather than about his personality, and about the sidelights they throw on the social and political tendencies of his age and of the time that was to come after him. "The past," says Carlyle, "is all holy to us," but Johnson makes the past not only holy, but, what is more to my purpose, actual. Through a wonderfully transparent medium there passes before us a human drama of singularly varied interest, the characters sharply defined, the plot strongly developed, the scenery picturesque, the *dénouement* tragically striking, and with a chief actor who holds us with his spell as firmly as the Ancient Mariner held his wedding guest. Much of this we owe to Boswell, but not all. Johnson impressed everybody, even those who hated him, and

[1] Reprinted by kind permission from the *Gentleman's Magazine*.

he left a good broad mark on the history of his time. Full of ideas, he became a sound, though limited, thinker, a good scholar, a great critic, and almost a great poet. Let us try and watch some of these ideas in their development, and see where they led Johnson, as well as what relations they had to contemporary thought.

Johnson began to be a notable figure in English literature about the middle of the eighteenth century. It was a poorish time to live in. English influence abroad was at its lowest. English morals were not high. English religion, soon to be clarified by the Evangelical revival, was getting very thick and dreggy. The social side is described in Fielding; its religious texture was supplied by writers like Pope, and was little more than Deism, with an easy, shallow, utilitarian basis. "Whatever was, was good"—including Anglican parsons who finished their sixth bottle under the dinner table. English literature, however, was not to be despised. Pope and Addison, Swift and Defoe, were no more; the great work of the three latter in laying the foundation of modern English prose was complete. But in their stead had arisen Richardson and Fielding, and were soon to arise Fanny Burney, and, later still, Jane Austen. We had the English comedy of manners, the English essay: we were to have the English novel. Greater work than this, however, was on foot. Bishop Berkeley had opened up a new world of mental vision and new avenues for philosophy. The work of Locke in clearing out old metaphysical lumber, and basing knowledge on experience, was to be continued by a greater than he. Butler, when Johnson was a young man, had confounded the Deists by showing that Nature was as cruel as the orthodox scheme which they condemned; the great Hume was soon to use Butler's argument, as he used Locke's philosophy, to buttress a still more advanced sceptical position, and Paley was to deliver the broadside of the orthodox party. But it was France, not England, that was the true seat of the great intellectual warfare of the eighteenth century, to which Carlyle has been so strangely indifferent. Voltaire was great when Johnson was comparatively unknown. Rousseau did his best work almost simultaneously with that of the English writer. Everywhere there were changes and the omens of change. What contribution did Johnson make to them? In order the better to answer this question, it is necessary to say a word of Johnson's personality.

You know it well. Carlyle was troubled with nerves and a stomach, and he let the world know it. Johnson's huge body was an accumulation of physical diseases equalled, I should say, by few and surpassed by none. He was half-deaf and more than half-blind; he was at times morbid to insanity; he had tendencies to palsy, gout, asthma, dropsy; his face was seamed with scrofula; he rarely passed a day without pain. His early life was unhappy and obscure. The ills of the scholar's life, which he enumerates in the immortal line:

"Toil, envy, want, the patron, and the gaol,"

he had known with one exception—he never had a patron. It was the era of free trade in literature, following on a period of thoroughly unhealthy protection. "A man," he said to Boswell, "goes to a bookseller, and gets what he can; we have done with patronage"; and the letter to Lord Chesterfield—the Magna Charta, as it was, of literary independence—simply stated the bare, hard facts of his career. The last thirty years of Johnson's life were secure from want, but the iron had entered into his soul. His character, built up as it was on severe and massive lines, took a permanently gloomy tinge. "The majority of mankind are wicked," was the old Greek text to which he preached many an impressive sermon. The man who had tramped about London with Savage, who had known what it was to go without food for two days, who had sat, a tame author, in Cave's closet, was not a man to join in the optimist's praise of the system of things. There is a piece of work of Johnson's which, in addition to being one of the most impressive combinations of satire and argument in the English language, fully explains his moral outlook. Soame Jenyns, outvying Pope, had written a jaunty tract on the origin of evil, which treated poverty and all the ills of life as proper and not unpleasing accidents in the general scheme, especially designed to bring out the goodness of the Creator and the virtues of His creatures. Partial evil was universal good, and so on. Johnson would have none of this. Poverty and crime were not things to be laid with rose-water. "Life," he said, "must be seen before it can be known." This author and Pope perhaps never saw the miseries which they imagine thus easy to be borne. "Pain," he said scornfully, "is useful to alarm us that we may shun greater evils, but those evils must be presupposed to exist that the fitness of pain may appear." But perhaps the wildest and silliest of Soame Jenyns' fancies was that all the sufferings of man were designed for the amusement and instruction of a superior order of creatures, who watched our contortions much as the angler views the writhings of the fish on his hook. Johnson ridiculed the idea that a set of beings unseen and unheard are "trying experiments on our sensibility, putting us in agonies to see our limbs quiver, torturing us to madness that they may laugh at our vagaries, sometimes obstructing the bile that they may see how a man looks when he is yellow, sometimes breaking a traveller's bone to see how he will get home, and sometimes killing him for the greater elegance of his hide." Least of all could Johnson imagine how men could talk and think lightly of death. He said with Claudio, "Death is a fearful thing." The horror of it shook him all his life through. As human existence was to him a state in which much was to be endured

and little to be enjoyed, so the end of it was to be
continually dreaded. He closed the series of "Idlers,"
a charming, and, on the whole, a cheerful series of
essays, with the remark, "The secret horror of the
last is inseparable from a thinking man, whose life is
limited, and to whom death is dreadful." "Is not the
fear of death natural to man?" asked Boswell. "So
much so," replied Johnson, "that the whole of life
is but keeping away the thoughts of it." There was
a morbid touch in this, and it throws into relief Johnson's love of company, his pathetic desire to have bright
and kind faces around him to ward off the grim spectre
he feared. But I dwell on it specially because it gives
the key to Johnson's religious fervour. He believed
and trembled. Much was mysterious; nearly all was
dark; faith was essential. God, he thought, with
Addison's Cato, willed the happiness of His creatures,
and as that happiness was imperfectly fulfilled in this
world, there was another where all would be well.
But for scepticism he would have none of it. He
abhorred sceptics even more than Whigs, and we all
know that the first Whig was the devil. Hume,
whom he probably did not read, must be a liar and a
scoundrel; and one of the worst quarrels he ever had
was with Adam Smith, for hinting that Hume was a
good man. "You lie, sir," said Johnson, with laconic
insolence; and Adam Smith's retort was rather worse
than its provocation. If a man got sceptical he should
look to his liver, or drink himself out of it. But he

himself was too real a creature altogether to banish the obstinate questionings which belonged to his age, and indeed none of his contemporaries seemed to realise them with so deep a sense of personal unhappiness. "I will have no more on't," he cried, in terrible agitation, as his friends discussed his and mankind's chances of salvation. "Treat life as a show, which man should cheerfully enjoy," it was suggested. "Yes, sir," replied Johnson, "if he is sure he is to be well after he goes out of it. But if he is to grow blind after he goes out of the show-room, and never to see anything again; or if he does not know whither he is to go next, a man will not go cheerfully out of a show-room." Indeed, if we are to take Carlyle's estimate of greatness, we must admit that Johnson, who was much troubled with the immensities, and the mysteries, and the "verities," was a great man.

Johnson, therefore, was religious in spite of himself. He would have said with Newman: "The whole world seems to give the lie to the great truth of the being of a God, and of that truth my whole being is full." But, as I have shown, he would have nothing to do with philosophic doubt. Nor would he turn Papist. "I have fear enough," he said, honestly, "but an obstinate rationality prevents me," and he would not treat a man, *à la* Pope, as a mere machine. But he did not care for transcendental guesses at the great secret. He took the traditional religion and ritual; he was neither mystic nor methody, and he sniffed scornfully at the idealist theory. "I refute it thus," he said—"it" being the non-existence of "matter"—striking his foot against a stone. He probably knew that he had not refuted "it" at all, but that was Johnson's short way with men and theories for which he had no taste. So with the free-will controversy. All theory might be against the freedom of the will. Johnson, with his way of testing all things by rough-and-ready experience, knew better. "We know our will is free, and there's an end on't," and for Mr. Boswell, of course—and a good many other people too—there *was* an end on't. Johnson's attitude towards politics was much of the same character. He had been called the last of the Tories; but he really was a Gallio, caring for none of these things, and saying generally that he would not give half a guinea to live under one form of government more than another. Johnson was a confirmed individualist. Patriotism he delicately denominated as the last refuge of a scoundrel, and politics were to him a mere game of the ins and outs, in which no sensible man, with books and good talk, and friends at his club, would dream of taking a hand. The Whigs he hated, for he thought they were opposed to all order, and theories of equality and natural rights were his *bêtes noires*. "Madam," he said to a fine lady democrat, a kind of she Horace Walpole, "I am now become a convert to your way of thinking. I am convinced that all mankind are upon an equal footing; and to give you an unquestionable proof, madam, that I am in earnest, here is a very sensible, civil, well-behaved fellow-citizen, your footman; I desire that he may be allowed to sit down and dine with us." He held there was a natural law against oppression. If kings got too tyrannical the people would cut off their heads. As for political squabbles: "Pooh! Leave me alone," he cried to a mob, roaring for Wilkes and liberty; "I, at least, am not ashamed to own that I care for neither the one nor the other." And he said profoundly of the whole controversy that to his mind a far worse thing than keeping Wilkes out of his parliamentary rights was that so many people wanted to have such a man in Parliament at all. We think of Tennyson—

> " He that roars for liberty,
> Faster binds the tyrant's power,"

and confess that here, too, as in many other things, Johnson's sturdy sense was right, more especially as, having the root of the matter in him, he saw that the end of government was not, as the cant of the Whigs went, the establishment of any fanciful system of political balance, but the social well-being of the whole people. What a wise saying is this, for instance: "A decent provision for the poor is the true test of civilisation. Gentlemen of education," he observed, "were pretty much the same in all countries; the condition of the lower orders, the poor especially, was the true mark of national discrimination." For

Ireland he had ever a good word. "When," said Boswell, "the corn laws were in agitation in Ireland, by which that country has been enabled not only to feed itself, but to export corn to a large amount, Sir Thomas Robinson observed that those laws might be prejudicial to the corn trade of England. 'Sir Thomas,' said he, 'you talk the language of a savage. What, sir! would you prevent any people from feeding themselves, if by any honest means they can do it?'"

Talking women, indeed, he hated, and, as he was a bit of a Turk in his way, I am afraid the shrieking sisterhood would have had short shrift from him. "Here," he said in his poem "London,"

> "Falling houses thunder on your head,
> And here a female atheist talks you dead."

Generally, one may say of Johnson that most of his vehement hatreds were inspired by his sensitiveness to humbug of all kinds, especially humbug masquerading as truth—truth beyond the common. Horace Walpole, who did not love the Doctor, said that Johnson had neither taste nor judgment, but only his old woman's prejudices. Perhaps Johnson was thinking of Walpole when he remarked of the men of feeling, "Sir, don't be duped by them any more. You will find these very feeling people are not very ready to do you good. They pay you by feeling." He certainly told a good average truth about human nature when he insisted in his depressing, but not cynical, way that the misfortunes of a friend—from hanging downwards—did not affect a man's appetite for dinner. "Sir," he said, "I should do what I could to bail him and give him any other assistance, but if he were once fairly hanged I should not suffer." Boswell: "Would you eat your dinner that day, sir?" Johnson: "Yes, sir; and eat it as if he were eating with me. Why, there's Baretti, who is to be tried for his life to-morrow; friends have risen up for him on every side; yet, if he should be hanged, none of them will eat a slice of pudding the less. Sir, that sympathetic feeling goes a very little way in depressing the mind."

Humanitarian as he was, he would not over-state his case. Marriages made in heaven? Nonsense! the Lord Chancellor might make them all, and no one would be a penny the worse. The luxury of the rich an evil? By no means. It did good and employed labour. Better for a man to spend £10,000 a year than to give away £8,000 and spend £2,000. "Clear your mind of cant"; "Don't pretend that the moral average is higher than it is"; "Trust God, and keep clear of liquor," was Johnson's recipe for superfine criticisms of life.

One would have thought that this touchstone of common-sense applied to literature would have produced splendid results. So in a sense it did. Johnson has contributed many imperishable sayings to the English language. Unfortunately, in literary matters he had a divided life. Macaulay has exaggerated the contrast between Johnson talking at his ease in the club or at Mrs. Thrale's tea-table, and Johnson penning "Ramblers" in the study. Still, there was a difference. Talk was to the Doctor the wine of life; it stirred his pulses, quickened his powerful but rather sluggish intellect, brought out his humour, drove off his besetting melancholy. Alone in Bolt Court, with blue devils, his pen lagged, and he produced, with some profoundly interesting work, a good deal of lumber. Though he raised the tone of the essay, he disimproved its form, as the masterly hand of Addison left it. The "Ramblers" and "Idlers," for instance, are, on the whole, failures, for want of the salt of personality which makes the club talks successes. "Rasselas" is almost charming, but it resembles a theatrical performance by Mr. and Mrs. Vincent Crummles and Company. One was all Crummles; the other is all Johnson. Pakuah, Imlac, Rasselas, and the rest, all wear knee-breeches and buckles; their speech bewrayeth them.. Here and there, especially in the "Idlers," there is a lively personal touch worthy of the *Spectator;* and weighty satire and vigorous criticisms of life are never wanting. As an example of the former, take the complaint of the husband whose wife was mad on what ladies vaguely call "work." "We have twice as many fire-screens as chimneys, and three quilts for every bed. She has boxes filled with knit garters and braided shoes. Kitty knows not at sixteen the difference between a Protestant and a Papist, because she has been employed three years in filling a side of a closet with a hanging that is to represent Cranmer in the flames. And Dolly, my eldest girl, is now unable to read a chapter in the Bible, having spent all the time which other children passed at school in working the interview between Solomon and the Queen of Sheba." For serious stuff, read the solemn talks at the end of "Rasselas," read "London," and the "Vanity of Human Wishes;" and read them, too, in the light of Johnson's terrible trials, his ill-health, his morbid temper, his darkened hours, and the noble fortitude of his later years.

As a critic Johnson is excellent—intelligent, shrewd, knowing—and his worth may be well gauged by comparing him with his contemporaries, and even with the critical school of the earlier years of the nineteenth century. He has been abused for his mistakes. What critic is without them? What about the Edinburgh Reviewers? How many of Francis Jeffrey's literary verdicts remain? I was reading an article the other day to show that not one was worth the paper it was written on. What will Carlyle's historical criticisms be worth fifty years hence? What are Mr. Froude's worth now? Of Johnson, it may be said that as he produced the best dictionary in an age when philology was in its infancy, so he was the best literary critic of an age when there was very little criticism to speak of.

Look at the stuff which passes for literary judgments with Horace Walpole, who was always sneering at Johnson's "tasteless pedantry"! Johnson was, in fact, a good deal better than his age and his prejudices. His training led him to admire the formal rhymes, the mechanical metres, the monotonous balance of Pope and his school. Much of this poetry, it has been said, was like the style of gardening, in which the designer, if he placed a statue in a summer-house in one corner, preserved what he called "symmetry" by another summer-house and another statue in the other. Johnson's common-sense broke through these and similar traditions, and so his "Lives of the Poets" are full of sound sentiment; and even when they are wrong, are often well, and always amusingly, wrong. He certainly said that some poorish lines in Congreve were better than the best things Shakespeare ever wrote, but then he pointed to the true source of Shakespeare's greatness, as the poet of truth and nature. "His story requires Romans and kings, but he thinks only on men." How modern this is, and much else in Johnson! Critics have built a reputation on a tithe of the sound things scattered up and down "The Lives of the Poets." Cowley's, Dryden's, and Milton's, in spite of the terrible "howler" about "Lycidas," are excellent, and as lively as a dinner-bell. Read them, and then say whether Johnson's fame as a critic was undeserved, or whether you would put him down from his literary throne. One confesses, of course, that he had shocking prejudices. His taste in kings was terrible. He thought Charles II. and Louis XIV. very fine gentlemen. I wonder what he would have thought of George IV., whom, when he was a little boy, he examined in Scripture history, expressing himself much pleased with the intelligence of the future king.

Johnson was no "mummer worshipper." "Why should a man clap a hump on his back and a lump on his leg, and call himself Richard III. ?" He sincerely envied Garrick his guineas, just as Goldsmith envied Johnson his fame and literary pre-eminence. But, alas, he was not disinterested! He had asked the fops to be silent, and the wits to be dumb, when his abysmal drama, "Irene," was being performed, and the fops and the wits had responded with what Johnson calls "partial catcalls." Outside his own language and literature his curiosity was small. He went to Paris, where Hume and Gibbon had drunk in the spirit of the age at great gulps, and saw nothing but a parcel of nuns and old women of both sexes. What this stout old friend of "law and order" would have said of the great upheaval which swallowed up Burke's "Whig" sympathies one shudders even to think. Bozzy's life would have been unbearable, for that poor gentleman was tainted with the accursed thing, Whiggery.

And so we are led once more from literature to character, and having done qualifying and expounding, we can see for a moment Johnson as he was, reflecting how in an age of superficial sentiment, but of a good deal of real hardness, this man overflowed with tenderness, with love of all defenceless things, of children and animals, with innocent gaiety, with true charity. What a capital companion he made for young men! I hope the old story of his midnight "frisk" with Beauclerk and Langton is fit for ears polite.

"One night, when Beauclerk and Langton had supped at a tavern in London, and sat till about three in the morning, it came into their heads to go and knock up Johnson, and see if they could prevail on him to join them in a ramble. They rapped violently at the door of his chambers in the Temple, till at last he appeared in his shirt, with his little black wig on the top of his head, instead of a night-cap, and a poker in his hand, imagining, probably, that some ruffians were coming to attack him. When he discovered who they were, and was told their errand, he smiled, and, with great good humour, agreed to their proposal. 'What, is it you, you dogs! I'll have a frisk with you.' He was soon dressed, and they sallied forth together into Covent Garden, where the greengrocers and fruiterers were beginning to arrange their hampers, just come in from the country."

Youth and gaiety were always sacred to Johnson. "Let women dress prettily," he said to Mrs. Thrale, "not in evil-looking gowns. You little creatures should never wear those sort of clothes; they are unsuitable in every way. What, have not all insects gay colours?"

His charities were unceasing; they were bounded only by his means, and sometimes not even by them; and then, *à la* Leigh Hunt, he would borrow of the handiest friend, without the formality of an I O U. Remember that he kept his sick and aged mother when he could barely keep himself.

"I am extremely sorry," he wrote to a creditor, "that we have encroached so much upon your forbearance with respect to the interest, which a great perplexity of affairs hindered me from thinking of with that attention that I ought, and which I am not immediately able to remit to you, but will pay it (I think £12) in two months. I look upon this, and on the future interest of that mortgage, as my own debt; and beg that you will be pleased to give me directions how to pay it, and not to mention it to my dear mother. If it be necessary to pay this in less time, I believe I can do it; but I take two months for certainty, and beg an answer whether you can allow me so much time."

Persons with lighter claim on his consideration were not forgotten.

"Dear sir," he wrote to a friend; "I have an old amanuensis in great distress. I have given what I think I can give, and begged till I cannot tell where to beg again. I put into his hands this morning four guineas. If you could collect three guineas more it would clear him from his present difficulty.—I am, sir, your most humble servant,

"SAM JOHNSON."

There is nothing more delightful in the whole of "Boswell" than the story of Johnson's refusal to accept an invitation to a good dinner because of a prior engagement to dine with Mrs. Williams, his half-blind, crusty old pensioner, and his persistence in the refusal till "Bozzy" went to Bolt Court and begged him off. His own account of his interview with a dying companion of his mother has often been told, but I will repeat it here:—

"*Sunday, October* 18, 1767.—Yesterday, October 17, at about ten in the morning, I took my leave for ever of my dear old friend Catherine Chambers, who came to live with my mother about 1724, and has been but little parted from us since. She buried my father, my brother, and my mother. She is now 58 years old.

"I desired all to withdraw, then told her that we were to part for ever; that as Christians we should part with prayer, and that I would, if she was willing, say a short prayer beside her. She expressed great desire to hear me, and held up her poor hands, as she lay in bed, with great fervour, while I prayed, kneeling by her.

"I then kissed her. She told me that to part was the greatest pain that she had ever felt, and that she hoped we should meet again in a better place. I expressed, with swelled eyes, and great emotion of tenderness, the same hopes. We kissed and parted. I humbly hope to meet again, and to part no more."

An occasion inspiring the deep personal sorrow that the severing of old ties always awoke in him, was the leave-taking of the house at Streatham, which, after Mrs. Thrale's second marriage, was no longer a home for him, and of the church where he had worshipped for so many years. "Templum valedixi cum osculo," he said pathetically. He did not bear the misfortunes and sicknesses of his last years with uniform patience, but he had reserves of Christian stoicism, characteristic of his age and of his temper, on which to draw, and they did not fail him at the last. His morbid terror of death was then faced and laid in the spirit of his own prayer, written many years earlier. Christian stoicism was, indeed, the characteristic note of Johnson's literary work and character. Beyond that he had no message to the world, no leading idea, no carefully elaborated or artfully developed theory of life.

DR. JOHNSON AND LICHFIELD

A Paper read before the Johnson Club

BY

G. H. RADFORD

JOHNSON'S BIRTHPLACE.

Dr. Johnson and Lichfield

Notwithstanding the recent researches of our brother, Oscar Browning, I incline to the old belief that Johnson was born at Lichfield. That Johnson himself had the old belief does not weigh with me unduly. He was mistaken (according to Brother Birkbeck Hill) about the birth-place of his mother; and may have been mistaken about his own, for though this was a matter within his experience, it was probably beyond the reach of his memory, abnormally retentive as that faculty was in him. We have other evidence. Johnson had a "rustic tongue" (in a sense different from that in which the words are used in "London: A Satire"), and the country of which his tongue gave trace was Lichfield, or at any rate Staffordshire. To the end of his days he said "theer" for *there* "wŏnce" for *once*, "poonch" for *punch*, and employed other provincial pronunciations, which his friends considered peculiar to Lichfield. It is not surprising that Johnson under these circumstances maintained that the Lichfield people spoke the purest English. This was a symptom of local patriotism, as was the apostrophe to Lichfield in the dictionary, under the word *Lich*, "salve magna parens"! When we add to Johnson's belief this bewrayal of his tongue, and the general opinion of his contemporaries, we come to the conclusion that there is a high probability (and Paley has taught us that in historical inquiry we can expect no more) that the Samuel Johnson who appears from the register of Saint Mary's, Lichfield, to have been baptized on the 7th September, 1709, was the man in whose name we are met together. So let Lichfield continue to be proud of being the birthplace and the scene of Johnson's earlier life, of having furnished the objects which first impressed his senses, and called forth his infant thoughts. But let her not be too proud. The mature hero, we are told, is the product of the original or embryonic hero and his environment. While we remember here that Lichfield was the environment, let us not forget that all high excellence is congenital. Falstaff was *born* with "something a round belly," Pope "lisped in numbers," and Mark Twain tells us that he could lie before he could stand. Johnson would still have been a colossal figure though fate had assigned him a meaner birthplace than Lichfield. In 1709 the population of Lichfield probably did not exceed 4,000, and it was no doubt a green and quiet country town, overshadowed by its cathedral; nevertheless a cheerful place with a high reputation for ale—a place where we know, on the authority of Johnson himself, that all the *decent* people got drunk every night, and were not thought the worse of by their decent neighbours; such a town as it is not easy to find the counterpart of, now that manners have decayed and populations have increased tenfold, and the habitations of men have encroached on the open country.

Michael Johnson was past fifty when he married Mistress Sarah Ford, a maiden of forty, and still older when he begot his eldest son, Samuel. The question has been raised whether the boy was called after his godfather, Samuel Swinfen, or after his maternal uncle, Samuel Ford. The answer is of little importance, nor would it matter if the child really got his name direct from that other Samuel who was the son of Elkanah and Hannah. Michael was a bookseller, and had been a churchwarden. In the shop the young Samuel found abundant and miscellaneous material to satisfy his thirst for literature, and the son of the churchwarden remained to the end "a most unshaken Church of England man." Michael taught his firstborn to swim in a stream by Lichfield, and the boy learned so well that he excited the admiration of the dippers at Brighthelmstone fifty years after. No doubt he also learned to ride on that horse on which the elder Johnson used to "ride away for orders" when domestic discussions made it unpleasant to remain longer at home. Samuel acquired "a good seat," and frequently in later life rode to hounds with Mr. Thrale, though he complained that the dogs had less sagacity than he could have prevailed on himself to believe; and the gentlemen often called on him not to ride over them. No praise (according to Mrs. Thrale) ever went so close to his heart as when he heard a sporting man call out: "Why, Johnson rides as well, for aught I see, as the most illiterate fellow in England." Andrew Johnson (Michael's brother) taught his nephew "the art of attack and defence by boxing," and the art was not useless to the great man in after-life. "I have beat many a fellow," said Johnson to Mrs. Thrale, after confirming the story of his flooring Tom Osborne, the bookseller.

From his father, Johnson intimates that he inherited the melancholy which afflicted him, and he no doubt also inherited from him his immense frame and his prodigious mental powers. But Johnson's mother earliest impressed his memory, and his gratitude was unbroken during his long life. Mrs. Johnson carried her child to London at the age of two to be touched by Queen Anne for the king's evil, and this event he dimly and with awe remembered. When he was three years old she took him to the christening of her second son, Nathaniel. She told him as he sat in her lap the story of Saint George and the Dragon, and she, too, taught him to read. He was satisfied with this manner of beginning education, and maintained that this was the only kind of reading that could please an infant. "Babies do not want," said he, "to hear about babies; they like to be told about giants and castles, and of somewhat which can stretch and stimulate their little minds." When Mrs. Thrale urged in reply the numerous editions of "Tommy Prudent" and "Goody Two-shoes," "Remember always," said he "that the parents buy the books, and that the children never read them."

But Mistress Johnson did not forget his religious instruction. She gave him when a child in bed with her such a vivid description of heaven and hell that he never forgot what was thus communicated to him for the first time. This may not have been good medicine for his constitutional melancholy, but the communication was well intended. She was always kind to him, and he remembered all his life how she had given him coffee she could ill afford, to gratify his appetite when a boy.

At eight years old little Samuel was sent to Dame Oliver's school at Lichfield. She was sufficiently learned to be able to read the black-letter, and she asked Johnson to borrow for her from his father a Bible in that character. Later he had for teacher Tom Brown, who published a spelling-book and dedicated it to the Universe. Then he went to the Lichfield school, and began to learn Latin with the usher, Mr. Hawkins, "a man very skilful in his little way." After two years of his teaching Johnson rose to be under the care of the head-master, Mr. Hunter. It is interesting to learn from one of his schoolfellows that Johnson's only failing at this time was that of *talking* and diverting other boys from their business. A year at Mr. Wentworth's school at Stourbridge brought him to the age of sixteen, and the close of his early education.

His experience at school does not seem to have been happy, but he was distinguished among his fellows, and learned there (what is as easily learned at school as in the world) that he was on a level with the minds of his time, and that by effort he could outstrip them all.

In his nineteenth year he went to Oxford, and remained at Pembroke College there probably little more than fifteen months. He spent his vacation at Lichfield, and came back thither after he could no longer remain at Oxford. It was poverty which compelled him to come home without taking his degree, but he brought with him a vast amount of learning. What he read *solidly* at Oxford was Greek, and what he read otherwise nobody knows. Before he entered at Pembroke he had read very widely. "Sir," said he to Boswell in 1763, "in my early years I read very hard. It is a sad reflection, but a true one, that I knew almost as much at eighteen as I do now." To Mr. Langton he said that his great period of study was from twelve to eighteen. His reading was extremely miscellaneous, and it was the hard reading of this early period of the books in his father's stock that filled his mind with the material that surprised his contemporaries when, later in life, he had become a great talker.

This brings us to a period when we naturally and irresistibly desire to hear of Johnson's love: "a passion which he who never felt never was happy, and he who laughs at never deserves to feel; a passion which has caused the change of Empires, and the loss of worlds; a passion which has inspired heroism and subdued avarice." It is just here that we most regret the lack of material for his early life. Not that we are without material; but we should like to have before us all the evidence that there ever was. His first love was Olivia Lloyd, who charmed him while he was at the school at Stourbridge. From Boswell's statement that she was a "young Quaker" it is clear that she was both beautiful and demure; and her very name is a melody. No wonder Johnson loved her, and his love was not inarticulate, for he told her so in what Boswell calls somewhat brutally "a copy of verses." These early verses have perished, and we cannot, alas! redeem them from oblivion by the sacrifice of say half a dozen mature "Ramblers." Olivia's radiance, however, faded, or was eclipsed by that of Edmund Hector's sister. She afterwards married a clergyman named Careless. Nearly fifty years after she first dazzled him he met her (then a widow), and there was some revival of the old tenderness. She took her old admirer under her care, and told him when he had

had enough tea. "If I had married her," he says, "it might have been as happy for me." There was another love, Mrs. Emmett, an actress, who at Lichfield Theatre played *Flora* in "Hob in the Well." It was probably when warmed by this flame that he hurled from the stage into the pit a man (and possibly a rival) who had appropriated his chair. Johnson was not *elegans formarum spectator*, and there must have been something in Mistress Emmett which entangled him in addition to her beauty. How far these emotions led him, and what was the history of these young hearts, it is difficult to ascertain. There were, no doubt, other loves too; and I implore my brethren to leave no stone unturned, and to follow every clue, however slight, which may lead to discovery in this direction. Johnson was in love three or four times, on his own confession, before that affection of the heart which led to his marriage with the widow Porter. It is extremely unlikely that a man who has been three or four times in love has been in love *only* three or four times. I can confidently appeal to the experience of my brethren in support of this opinion. That Johnson does not speak freely about his early loves in general is no argument that he had only three or four. We are, unfortunately, dependent for our knowledge of Johnson's early life on his own statements—statements made to sincere admirers during the last twenty years of his life, when the early flames had cooled down or gone out in ashes. It was in this serene evening of life, and after Johnson had established a character as the " majestick teacher of moral and religious wisdom " that the confessions were made, and I strongly suspect that the confessions bore but a small proportion to the sins unconfessed. There is in Johnson's character and habits ground for this suspicion. Perhaps nothing is more frequently censured by him than indiscreet communicativeness. "A man should be careful," says he, " not to tell tales of himself to his own disadvantage"; and, assuming of Johnson what the porter of Trinity said of Byron, that he was "a young gentleman of tumultuous passions," nothing could be more embarrassing to a "majestick teacher of moral and religious wisdom" than a full disclosure of his adventures during those days when youth is inflammable and ignites at a touch. He heartily ridiculed Garrick, Goldsmith, Tom Osborne, and others, who freely told tales about themselves which a man of Johnson's discretion would not have revealed under torture. "What a monkey was David now, to tell of his own disgrace!" "He was a blockhead and told of it," says Johnson, speaking of Tom Osborne. "See now," he says on another occasion, "what haste people are in to be hooted!" Johnson was *not* in haste to be hooted, and he preferred a discreet reticence on everything which might discredit the "majestick teacher." He was right, as in matters of common-sense he invariably was; but we differ in some respects from his contemporary admirers, and should not think him discredited if he had (as I am inclined to believe) as many loves as Robert Burns, or the warmest of our Brethren. This subject is to us of special importance. The life of Johnson has been collected mainly from his sayings; the fund that has not been drawn on by his biographers is Johnson's *reticences*. That there were such is to be inferred from the passages quoted above, and from many others; and it is the duty of our diligent Brethren to explore and supply these reticences. Perhaps the best thing with which to fill up these gaps is evidence; but it is hardly to be hoped that we, following so many mighty gleaners, can collect much. Failing evidence, we must rely on the *a priori* method, and the problem to grapple with is this: given the character of Johnson, ascertain what he did under circumstances which he was too discreet to disclose. This method requires a profound knowledge of Johnson, and a nice and sound judgment. If applied at large there would be risk of failure and falsity, but entrusted solely to the Brethren, I anticipate from the method results at the same time considerable and surprising. And it is not unimportant for us to break new ground. We meet from time to time, and one of the Brethren, having reverently kissed the cup, hands round a draught drawn from the great well sunk by Boswell, and embellished and re-excavated by Brother Birkbeck Hill. There is no fear of the store being exhausted, but there seems a danger that the fare may become as familiar to us as water is said to be to teetotalers.

DR. JOHNSON AND LICHFIELD

But to return from this digression. After love comes not unfrequently marriage, and Johnson was married on the 9th day of July, 1735. He did not find his bride at Lichfield, but he brought her home thither. She was Mrs. Elizabeth Porter, the widow of a mercer at Birmingham, and twenty years older than the bridegroom, who was then nearly six-and-twenty. It was no abstract preference for widows which impelled Johnson on this occasion, for we find him saying in reference to the marriage of another: "He has done a very foolish thing, Sir; he has married a widow, when he might have had a maid."

Johnson took a house at Edial, near Lichfield, and set up a school, or endeavoured to do so. His advertisement in the *Gentleman's Magazine* that "at Edial, near Lichfield, in Staffordshire, young gentlemen are boarded and taught the Latin and Greek languages by Samuel Johnson," did not do much for him. He got however, some local support. David Garrick and his brother George, and a young gentleman named Offeley appear to have been his only pupils. Keeping a school was not an occupation for which Johnson was fitted, or in which he took any pleasure; and after carrying on the enterprise for some twelve months and dissipating most of the £800 which his wife brought him, he left Lichfield in 1737, and went to London "to drive the world about a little." From this date till the winter of 1761-2 Lichfield saw him no more. No indifference to his old haunts and his old friends is to be inferred from this long absence. Johnson had not chosen as he advised others to choose, " some business where much money may be got, and little virtue risked." On the contrary, he was living by his pen, and his life was a desperate and uncertain struggle with poverty and publishers. The stage coach from London took at least twenty hours in running to Lichfield, and the fare was four guineas. For many years it is improbable that Johnson was master at once of the time and the money necessary for such a journey. When at last he came back to his native place, he was famous. By his " London," his " Vanity of Human Wishes," " The Rambler," and the Dictionary, he had obtained acknowledged eminence as a man of letters. But his visit was not without sadness. He says, writing to Baretti on the 20th July, 1762 : " Last winter I went down to my native town, where I found the streets much narrower and shorter than I thought I had left them, inhabited by a new race of people, to whom I was very little known. My playfellows were grown old, and forced me to suspect that I was no longer young. My only remaining friend has changed his principles, and was become the tool of the predominant faction. My daughter-in-law " (the lexicographer should have written step-daughter) " from whom I expected most, and whom I met with sincere benevolence, has lost the beauty and gaiety of youth without having gained much of the wisdom of age. I wandered about for five days and took the first convenient opportunity of returning to a place where, if there is not much happiness, there is at least such a diversity of good and evil that slight vexations do not fix upon the heart."

This letter breathes the impatience of a middle-aged man not yet reconciled to destiny and inexorable change. Later on we shall find him at Lichfield, in a state more approaching resignation, treasuring the old friends that still remained, and the relics that revived early associations. From this time forward Johnson had no pecuniary difficulty in the way of travelling, for in June, 1762, Lord Bute did something to redeem a name otherwise ignoble, by granting Johnson a pension of £300 a year. During the remaining years of his life Johnson made at least eleven visits to Lichfield, generally in the summer or autumn, and often yearly, for several consecutive years. He was observant of and interested in every change, and his letters to Mrs. Thrale contain many local particulars collected as he rambled *inter fontes et flumina nota*. He writes her on the 14th August, 1769: "They have cut down the trees in George Lane. Evelyn, in his 'Book of Forest Trees,' tells us of wicked men that cut down trees, and never prospered afterwards; yet nothing has deterred these audacious aldermen from violating the hamadryads of George Lane. As an impartial traveller, I must however tell, that in Stow Street, where I left a draw-well, I have found a pump; but the lading-well in this ill-fated George Lane lies shamefully neglected."

Then he writes of Stow-pool and Borrowcop Hill, and places which are mere names to his correspondent, but of interest to him. Again he expresses his regret that "they have cut down another tree," and in other letters gives critical opinions on the state of the crops, and the strawberries and cherries with which his ladies fed him. His sojourn at Lichfield was *the* event of the year for his ladies, a number of gentle and cultured old souls, who entertained him heartily. There was (besides Lucy Porter), Mrs. Aston, Mrs. Cobb, Mrs. Adey, and many more, whom he never failed to visit. Men too, old school-fellows, whom he treated with tenderness, and whose deaths from time to time he sadly records. Old friends and acquaintances, with whom perhaps he played before he went to school, one of whom told him in 1771 that he had had *a matter of four wives*, " for which," says he to Mrs. Thrale, with singular mildness, "neither you nor I like him much the better."

To these Lichfield friends Johnson introduced from time to time both Boswell and the Thrales, and showed a dignified satisfaction in bringing together his town and country comrades. "Boswell is a favourite," he writes Mrs. Thrale, and he also tells her how much she is admired by the good people of Lichfield. Boswell tells us that Johnson was spoken of there not only with veneration but affection. All this is very natural. But seeing what men, and particularly literary men, are, it is pleasant to observe that

DR. JOHNSON AND LICHFIELD

just as Johnson could ride as well as the most illiterate fellow in England, so his relations with his native city and with the friends of his youth were as cordial as if he had never combined the parts of poet, journalist, and lexicographer.

Johnson was welcomed at Lichfield not only by old friends and other private citizens. The city in its corporate capacity was anxious to do honour to him, and this anxiety was displayed in a highly practical manner.

"On the 15th August, 1767, at a common hall of the bailiffs and citizens, it was ordered (and that without any solicitation) that a lease should be granted to Samuel Johnson, Doctor of Laws, of the encroachments at his house for the term of ninety-nine years, at the old rent, which was 5s., of which, as town-clerk, Mr. Simpson had the honour and pleasure of informing him, and that he was desired to accept without paying any fine on the occasion, which lease was afterwards granted, and the Doctor died possessed of this property." There are no doubt some pestilent Radicals who will blame the corporation of Lichfield for thus alienating public property at a nominal rent: preferring, in fact, to the public good, the good of Samuel Johnson. We admit that the corporation acted wrongly, and we applaud them for it. That man is not truly in love who develops scruples about the Decalogue while engaged in his mistress's service, and we might doubt the sincerity of Lichfield's esteem for Johnson if the corporation had been guided in this matter solely by considerations of high municipal policy.

We need not extend our subject so as to bring us to Johnson's last hours, but the latest visit to Lichfield ended in November, 1784, the month before his death. He was then, as he wrote to Sir John Hawkins, "relapsing into the dropsy very fast." That he did not die in the place where he was born and where his father, mother, and only brother were buried, is due to his wish to secure in London the advice of the best physicians. The last lines he wrote at Lichfield, addressed to two of his ladies, Mrs. Aston and Mrs. Gaswell, are these melancholy ones : " Mr. Johnson sends his compliments to the ladies at Stowhill, of whom he would have taken a more formal leave, but that he was willing to spare a ceremony which he hopes would have been no pleasure to them and would have been painful to himself."

DR. JOHNSON AND MUSIC

A Paper read before the Johnson Club

BY

JOHN SARGEAUNT

JOHNSON'S PEW IN ST. CLEMENT DANE'S CHURCH.

[To face p. 173.

Dr. Johnson and Music

WHEN a man takes in hand to defend himself against an unshapen accusation, his wisdom may well be doubted. It is related that in the Court of George I. it came to the ears of Madame de Kielmansegge that there were whispers against her reputation. Thereupon she obtained from her husband a signed and sealed declaration of his confidence in her faithfulness, and solemnly laid it at the feet of Princess Caroline. In the same Court the malice of an unsuccessful rival set going an evil report concerning Lady Cowper. When the report reached the ears of the gentle Countess she told her mistress that she should not deign to make any answer to the calumny. The Princess inferred the guilt of the Kielmansegge and the innocence of Lady Cowper, and posterity has accepted her verdict.

Death makes a difference, and the peculiarity of the

charge which it is now proposed to meet is, that it is brought against a hero by his worshipper, against a man of letters by his unwearied exponent, against Samuel Johnson by George Birkbeck Hill.

Lest there be any mistake in the matter, it is needful to transcribe the note. Johnson, says Dr. Hill, "had been wont to speak slightingly of music and musicians." The first symptom that he showed of a tendency to conversion was upon hearing the following read aloud from the preface to Dr. Burney's "History of Music," while it was yet in manuscript: " The love of lengthened tones and modulated sounds seems a passion implanted in human nature throughout the globe, as we hear of no people, however wild and savage in other particulars, who have not music of some kind or other, with which they seem greatly delighted." "Sir," cried Dr. Johnson after a little pause, "this assertion I believe may be right." And then, see-sawing a minute or two on his chair, he forcibly added: "All animated nature loves music—except myself!" Hawkins says that Johnson said of music, "It excites in my mind no ideas, and hinders me from contemplating my own." In Hawkins' mind Johnson sometimes excited the true notion that music was positive pain to him. Upon his hearing a celebrated performer go through a hard composition, and hearing it remarked that it was very difficult, he said, "I would it had been impossible." Yet he had once bought a flageolet, though he had never made out a tune. "Had I learnt to fiddle," he said, "I should have done nothing else." Not six months before his death he asked Dr. Burney to teach him the scale of music. That "he appeared fond of the bagpipe and used often to stand for some time with his ear close to the great drone" does not tell for much either way. In his "Hebrides" he shows his pleasure in singing. "After supper," he writes, "the ladies sung Erse songs, to which I listened, as an English audience to an Italian opera, delighted with the sound of words which I did not understand." Boswell records in the "Tour to the Hebrides," that another day "a lady pleased him much by singing Erse songs and playing on the guitar." Johnson himself shows that if his ear was dull to music, it was by no means dead to sound. He thus describes a journey by night in the wilds of the Highlands: "The wind was loud, the rain was heavy, and the whistling of the blast, the fall of the shower, the rush of the cataracts, and the roar of the torrent, made a nobler chorus of the rough music of nature than it had ever been my chance to hear before." In 1783, when he was in his seventy-fourth year, he said on hearing the music of a funeral procession: "This is the first time that I have ever been affected by musical sounds."

Now, it must be confessed that Dr. Hill is not very explicit in his accusation. The libel is obscurely hinted at by one who is conscious of its enormity and uncertain of its truth, yet a careful reader cannot fail to see the implication that Johnson altered or might have altered his views on music, that he was coming to tolerate, nay, even to approve of it. I shall try to prove that there is no warrant for this grave charge, that there were no signs of dotage in Johnson's declining years, that he deliberately formed and consistently maintained the belief that music is in itself a triviality, occasionally rising to the dignity of a nuisance; and I shall suggest that had his years been prolonged into our own time, when, musicians have commenced our lords, when, although to any reasonable intent speechless themselves, they labour to take away the freedom of speech from an oppressed and deafened minority, he would not have been content with an occasional word of slight, but would have taken the field against this bristling enemy, as no more destructive of the peace than dangerous to the faith, the reason, and the morals of the world.

Let us then examine Dr. Hill's evidence, and adduce such other testimony as may be found. To his first witness we cannot listen for a moment. She was tainted in her birth and corrupt in her education. Whatever respect we may feel for the creator of the Branghtons we cannot forget that she was Dr. Burney's daughter. A generous weakness may even pardon misrepresentations which were due to filial piety. Johnson, who defined politeness as "fictitious benevolence," looked upon himself as a very polite man, and yet in Dr. Burney's presence he assailed at some length the art to which Burney had misdevoted his life. Contrast this with the treatment he accorded to Wilkes under the hospitable roof in the Poultry. What other inference is possible than that he regarded the works of Burney as potentially more dangerous than the works of the great agitator and obscene commentator, who helped him to veal and lemon at Dilly's? In these circumstances what could a dutiful daughter do but gloss the truth? If, indeed, she could have foreseen that her lightly-written words would have been deliberately quoted with a view to casting aspersions upon Johnson's character, she might have let her father and his art go to the wall. And after all, if we accept the good lady's testimony, what does it amount to? A passage was read which was intended to prove that the love of music, like, as we may add, the love of picking and stealing, is universally implanted in man. The writer used the word "universally" in a chorographical sense; else Johnson might have pointed out that a first Whig had done his wicked work in Eden ere Jubal, in Charles Lamb's phrase, "stumbled upon the gamut." As it was, the poor savage, the bearer of many fardels, has another put on his shoulders, and no doubt he has an excuse and an appropriate occasion which we cannot plead. Music gives time to the dance which he performs round the bones of his enemies, and so assists him to digest their flesh. Johnson did not accept Burney's assertion; he only said it *might* be true. As he "always expressed a preference for civilised over uncivilised life," he was not likely to listen to the savage; and we shall find little difficulty in forgiving his somewhat haughty and exaggerated boast that all animated nature loved music except himself. The statement that he expressed a willingness to have a new sense put into him rests on the authority of the Burneys only; and the father's version differs from the daughter's. Even if it were true, it would but show the polite complaisance of fictitious benevolence.

The next piece of evidence is likewise Burney's. He says that Johnson not six months before his death expressed a wish to be taught the scale. Now, it is not pretended that any steps were taken to instruct him in this alphabet of music. Dr. Burney has put himself between the two stools of mendacity and unkindness. In fact, Johnson's wish was no more real than the man's who says he should like to commit a murder in order to know what a murderer feels like; while at seventy-four he may well have felt that the period of his remorse would be exceeding brief.

Then he bought a flageolet. It is cruel to bring up against a man the sins of his salad days. It is true that the offence cannot in itself be pardoned, but it may be said in mitigation, that he never made out a tune on the instrument. It is not positively asserted that he ever tried. His picking up such a relic of barbarism as a flageolet may deprive him of a claim to that evangelical virtue which he ascribed to

DR. JOHNSON AND MUSIC

Langton, but it will at least leave him on the level of his other good friend whom he suspected of not scrupling to pick up a certain offshoot or bywork of civilisation which is unhappily still extant.

Even Macaulay, who in spite of his Philistinism, was practically sound upon this question, is recorded to have once recognised a tune. In that case casuistry and politics combined to assist what is absurdly called the ear. He had to reflect that even a Whig had learnt a lesson from a Jesuit, that the clan of Maccallum More had done evil that good might come, and in order to drive the malignants before them had raised the terrific strains of "The Campbells are Coming."

Dr. Hill is candid enough to quote what Johnson said of Newbery's fiddle. "Young man, give the fiddle to the first beggar man you meet or you will never be a scholar." To the charge that he was affected by the music which he heard in the Hebrides he has himself supplied the answer. The tour to the Hebrides was in 1773, and ten years later, when he heard the music of a funeral procession, he said it was the first time he had ever been affected by musical sounds. Doubtless it was the ladies of the isles that pleased the amorous old man, and not the music they made. As for the funeral music, it may be suspected that Langton was moralising on death, and Johnson, who loathed the subject, diverted him by a startling fiction.

I have heard two other pieces of evidence alleged

on this point, to wit, that Johnson called his college a nest of singing birds, and that he wrote a musician's epitaph. Well, "London" and the "Vanity of Human Wishes" are among the songs of that aviary; but who would dare to set them to music? The complimentary epitaph on Philips is ascribed to Johnson by Garrick, to Garrick by others. It first appeared with the signature G. Another celebrated poem appeared in a lady's magazine and was signed with an L and eight stars. We have Pitt's authority for saying that analogy will prove anything, and the mere absence of stars will not prevent us from asserting that this epitaph was as certainly Garrick's as the "Expiring Frog" was undoubtedly Mrs. Leo Hunter's. And then an epitaph! We may imagine that Johnson would have been charmed to write epitaphs for the whole musical race if such condescension would accelerate their claims to possess them. To my shame I know a clergyman who was wroth with his clerk for tolling the bell at a Dissenter's funeral. "I believe," he said, "that for sixpence you'd toll for the devil." "Sir," said the clerk, "I'd do it for nowt." And this is the flimsy and interested testimony on which the case against Johnson rests. Now, look at the evidence on the other side. Dr. Hill has quoted some, but there is plenty more. Look at the bitter complaint in "London":

"Warbling eunuchs fill our silenced stage,"

in which line I take the indignant emphasis to be rather on warbling than on the word which it qualifies. Look at the iniquities of the resident alien,

> "They sing, they dance, clean shoes,"

and the rest. The cleaning of shoes is a reputable employ, and I have always been at a loss to understand what it did in this galley.

Johnson compared fiddling with knitting, of which at another time he said that it was to be reckoned next to mere nothing in the scale of insignificance. He held fiddling a bar to virtue, for "a man would never undertake great things could he be amused with small." He had seen fine fiddlers whom he "liked as little as toads." Bet Flint, of whom he "used to say that she was generally slut and drunkard, occasionally whore and thief," crowned her crimes by possessing "a spinnet on which she played." If a spirit of quibbling should lead any one to point out that Johnson's exact words were "occasionally whore and thief, she had, *however*, a spinnet," he must be told of the obvious meaning that her possession of a spinnet made one expect that she would not have been an occasional sojourner in the region of prostitution and robbery, but would have had there a legal domicile and a permanent home. "Would not," he asked, "a man be disgraced by singing publicly for hire? No, sir, there can be no doubt here. I know not if I should not prepare myself for a public singer as readily as let my wife be one." Again, he cried to Boswell, "Do you respect a rope-dancer or a ballad-singer?" He could indeed be got to the oratorio, and Mrs. Thrale might flatter herself he was listening, but to listening he could not be brought. He was composing Latin verses, and indignantly addressing himself:

> "Tene mulceri fidibus canoris?
> Tene cantorum modulis stupere?"

He could be got to write a dedication for music for the German flute, knowing, wise man, that there were no surer means of destroying music than that melancholy instrument. At St. Asaph he noted, with undoubted if unexpressed approval, that the service was sung only in the psalms and hymns. He could not away with Boswell, when he was fain to make the Handel Festival an excuse for not accompanying him. Above all, he could not away with Mrs. Thrale's desire to forget the fair mountain of her first husband and batten on the moor of an Italian music master. He would have nothing to do with a "method of employing the mind without the labour of thinking at all, and with some applause from a man's self." If he was forced to listen to Erse songs he sought consolation in trying to find their meaning, and found it in finding they had none, no more indeed than the "Radaratoo, radarate, radara tadara tandore," that he had heard in his childhood. One trembles to

DR. JOHNSON AND MUSIC

think of the consequences if McLeod of Ulinish had said to his face what he avowed behind his back. "It is music to hear this man speak." Ulinish would have blanched before the storm, as poor Mr. Pepys blanched at Streatham. Moreover, Johnson's staff had not yet disappeared in the timberless Mull. There are some indications that Boswell, after his wont, was too far in his cups to hear aright what Ulinish said. After the publication of this statement a contemporary might have appealed, on this as on other points, from Boswell drunk to Boswell sober; but it must be remembered that after Johnson's death the sittings of the higher judge grew ever less frequent, till they ended in a perennial vacation.

Finally, in Johnson's ideal college many arts had their representatives, but there was to be no teacher of music. If he regarded music as a trifle in his days, what would he have said now? Every one will remember the magnificent, if unconscious, encomium which Newman bestowed upon us, "It is not at all easy, humanly speaking, to wind up an Englishman to a dogmatic level." It has not been easy to convince the sturdy Englishman that his destiny was to become a piece of musical machinery, and to be wound up by a key to Handel or Wagner. He used to hold that music was the amusement of the weaker creature, male or female. The flute for Dick Swiveller, and Dick Swiveller for the flute. There used to be "old swearing" if a man's neighbour hammered on the fragments of an elephant's tusk or worried a cat's inside with a horse's tail. Now, like the place of the stomach, all this is changed. We are told that an aged statesman once sang nigger breakdowns, and we hear it without a blush; that a younger minister gives two hours daily to the piano, and yet we trust to him the destinies of our nation. The ministers of yore had their faults. Walpole talked bawdy, Newcastle slobbered, Fox gambled, Pitt drank. Some had two wives, some had none. Yet which of them sank so low as this? We have seen a flood of what Mill called "weak convictions, paralysed intellects, and growing laxity of opinions." We have heard this flood attributed—oh, worst outrage of all—to the rising tide of democracy. We have ignored the fact that it may be traced in every particular by logical and chronological sequence by inference irrefragable and deduction irresistible, to the bursting of the cesspools of music, and we wade complacently in the oozy sludges of our doom. And this is the hour when Dr. Hill suggests that Johnson might have become a musician. And yet Dr. Hill must have known very well that music was the cause of Johnson's hypochondria and excessive fear of death. He once told Boswell with bitter irony that music might make part of our future felicity. In fact, he had been reared in the current faith; he looked to a material heaven and a material hell—but what a heaven! and what a hell! what an alternative for a reasoning immortal! a choice between Scylla and Charybdis, between the devil and the deep sea, between an eternity of fire and an eternity of music.

There seems to be no record of any occasion on which Hawkins or Burney made in Johnson's hearing any serious defence of the art in whose service they spent such faculties as they possessed. Yet, as the nature of evil is always the same, we may conjecture after what fashion such defence was made. It were cruel to reproach the musician that he cannot answer in his own tongue, that herein he has no profit of his quavers and semiquavers, his fugues and toccatas, diminuendo and crescendo. Yet doubtless then, as now, his lack of articulation led him to call in the aid of an alien art, to appeal to authority, to take blank verse for argument, and cull you lines from the poets. He would tell you of Dryden writing odes to St. Cecilia, and of the diapason closing full in man, and he would ignore Dryden's sly hint that the creation of man should have put an end to music. He could not then, as his successors do, hunt for music in Mrs. Cowden Clarke's concordance to Shakespeare, but doubtless in some less nefarious way he laid hold of the lines in which Lorenzo assailed the unmusical.

> "The man that hath no music in himself,
>   Nor is not moved with concord of sweet sounds,
>   Is fit for treasons, stratagems, and spoils."

With what bludgeoning of polysyllables would

Johnson have received such specious argument. No, sir, Shakespeare is no more responsible for Lorenzo's mendacity than for Iago's insinuations or Macbeth's midnight murder. And who was Lorenzo, forsooth, that a man should listen to him? A knave very voluble, who caught the casket thrown from Shylock's window, *non rapuit sed recepit,* the receiver who is worse than the thief, a midnight eloper compassing his salt and most hidden loose affection, and saved from justice by unjust laws. Verily we must have better security than Lorenzo's. It were better to look for authority to him whom the Senate deemed "all-in-all sufficient," and who cared not for any music save that which might not be heard; an excellent kind and worthy of all commendation. If Lorenzo were worthy an answer we might take pattern from Sir Oliver Surface. As that little nabob met all objections to his nephew's character with the refrain, "But he wouldn't sell my picture," so we might say, "But Charles Lamb had no ear."

When in the year 1697 the curtain of Drury Lane rose upon the beautiful Bracegirdle enacting the part of the woful Princess of Granada, what musician in the audience but was eager to applaud Almeria when she avowed that

> "Music hath charms to soothe a savage breast,
> To soften rocks or bend a knotted oak."

Of all who have since taken the trouble to quote or

misquote the lines, how many have reflected that we have nought to do with savage breasts, or known that poor Almeria went on to remark that, despite this effect upon the savage and the inanimate creation, music was powerless to do aught for herself? The modern musician is fond of tossing about a line of Tennyson which speaks of "perfect music wed to noble words," and he fails to see that the very epithet applied to music is destructive of his case. The only things worth attempting in this world are those which cannot be done. The only worthy ideal is that which cannot be realised. If music admits of perfection it is unworthy the serious energising of man.

Charles Lamb called an oratorio a "profanation of the purposes of the cheerful playhouse," and if poor poetry is thus to be wrested from its sense it were better we were all like the German pedagogue who was asked to explain two lines of Shelley. He glanced at the book and handed it back, saying, "Ach ! it 'ave no meaning. It is boedry."

It was perhaps some reminiscence of Congreve that led the appalling collector of "A Million Facts" to allege in favour of music that it had a soothing effect upon the hippopotamus. Johnson, asked by a west-countryman whether he were a botanist, replied, "No, sir, I am not a botanist; and, should I wish to become a botanist, I must first turn myself into a reptile." It is conceivable that Johnson would have had no objection to music had a fatherly legislation enjoined that every musician should first become a hippopotamus. Then, indeed, it were needless for a suffering class to echo Charles Lamb's plaintive cry:

> "Some cry up Haydn, some Mozart,
> Just as the whim bites; for my part
> I do not care a farthing candle
> For either of them, or for Handel,—
> Cannot a man live free and easy
> Without admiring Pergolesi?
> Or through the world with comfort go
> That never heard of Dr. Blow?"

Then it were needless to feel again the woful longing that oppressed Johnson. "I would it had been impossible." Few of us have Johnson's courage.

> "The lion needs but roar to guard his young,
> The lapwing lies, says 'here' when they are there."

We feebly simper applause, we cull honeyed epithets from the garden of hypocrisy, and crown the musician with flowers that, like poor Bruno's in the fairy tale, are but a phlizz. In vain is it pretended that the goddess of music dwelt in maiden meditation on Parnassus' peak. In sooth she was debauched long agone, and, becoming the mother of Hypocrisy, found herself in turn the grandmother of the other vices. Knowing this, Johnson may well have declared that the nonjurors could not reason when he found one of them defending the use of instrumental music in public worship on the ground that the notes of the organ had a power to counteract the influence of devils on the spinal marrow of human beings, for the spinal marrow when decomposed became a serpent. Johnson did indeed once prescribe drunkenness as a remedy for unhappiness, but this seems scarcely to commend music as a remedy for devils, unless, indeed, we are willing to accept the principles of homœopathy.

Let us hear the conclusion of the whole matter. Johnson, like the Greeks, was an idealist, and therefore breathed inspiration into every form of honest thought, and lends strength to every form of manly energy. The Whig and the Tory, the Oligarch and the Radical, the Catholic and the Agnostic, sit at his feet. Burke and Boswell were of his friends; Macaulay and Stephen of his worshippers. Even bad men unlearn some of their badness in his presence, for Croker's treatment of Cochrane justifies all that Macaulay said of his enemy. Of those who profess to aspire after righteousness the musician only can find no help from Johnson. What can we infer save that his profession is idle and empty? The wicked finds no cover for his wickedness, the fool no cover for his folly, the musician no cover for his music. When the present wave of evil has spent its strength the true Englishman will again emerge. He will marvel how he came to be swept away, and he will see that not without reason was Johnson at once the reformer of morals and the enemy of music.

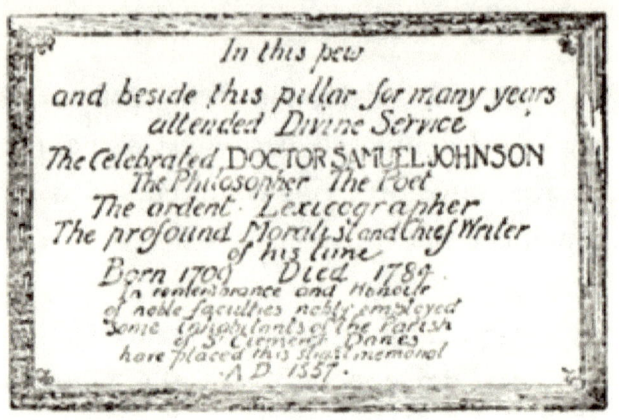

INSCRIPTION ON THE PEW IN ST. CLEMENT DANES.

DR. JOHNSON'S POLITICS

A Paper read before the Johnson Club
by
JOHN SARGEAUNT

THE COCK TAVERN DOORWAY ON THE NORTH SIDE OF FLEET STREET (NOW PULLED DOWN.)

[To face p. 193

Dr. Johnson's Politics

"Johnson, though a bigoted Tory," says Macaulay, "was not quite such a fool" as Croker would make him. In fact, Macaulay's restriction is somewhat superficial and demands much limitation. An attempt may perhaps be made to prove that the opposite statement is nearer to truth, that in fact Johnson was a Whig. His Toryism was carried on his sleeve, but it was too abstract and too conventional to be quite genuine. Every one knows his sayings that the first Whig was the devil; that in his Parliamentary reports he took care that the Whig dogs did not get the best of it; that Burke was a cursed Whig, a bottomless Whig. What is there on the other side? Whigs and Tories were originally distinguished quite as much by ecclesiastical differences, by the bent of religion, as by politics. To the Tory a clergyman was an object of reverence, to the Whig of suspicion. The Lichfield bookseller, Johnson's father, was a Tory, but took the oaths, and his son's views of the non-jurors were as contemptuous as any Whig's. In theory he was a Tory; in practice, hard experience dealing with the individual often made him a Whig. He wished the clergy to have considerable influence founded upon the opinion of mankind, but could not raise his own opinion of them to the requisite height. The Tory sat at their feet; Johnson was critical and often cold. Goldsmith took his religion from the priest as he took his coat from the tailor. "Sir," said Johnson, "he knows nothing; he has made up his mind about nothing." If nothing could make Johnson contradict a bishop, in practice he often did worse. He could sneer at Archbishop Secker and call Bishop Newton a gross flatterer. He went near to calling Bishop Keppel a whited wall, and Boswell is forced to surmise that he wist not it was the High Priest. Bishops *in posse*, deans and the like, were always suffering at his hands. Percy was driven from the table, Douglas tossed and gored, and Barnard forced to defend himself with a biting epigram. Worse than all, when Johnson was for founding an ideal university, he named no clergyman among his professors. He would trust theology to nobody but himself. On remonstrance he tossed practical divinity to Percy, throwing British antiquities in with it, and reserved theology as a science to himself. It is true that the professorships were to be limited to members of the club; but what living clergyman would Johnson have set above Percy? He would have faced a battery of cannon to restore Convocation to its full powers, but we feel that he would have had scanty respect for its ordinances. It is true that the bishops of his later life were chiefly Whigs, most of them, indeed, those creatures of the Duke of Newcastle who deserted him on his fall, and for once made him a wit. "Even Fathers in God," said the old minister, "sometimes forget their maker." But even Johnson's own Tory divines were little to his mind. The ideal of a Tory bishop was Atterbury, yet he is mentioned but once, and that inevitably, in all Johnson's writings. Nor does he figure more in Boswell's biography. Possibly Atterbury's Jacobitism may have been outweighed in Johnson's eyes by the force of language with which he expressed it. Bishop of Rochester and Dean of Westminster though he was, "D——n it," he said, when Queen Anne died, "d——n it, there's not a moment to lose." The same objection may have lain against Swift, to whom Johnson would allow neither head nor heart. All his reverence went out toward Usher, of whom it was said that, had all churchmen been like him, there had been no Nonconformity. For a Nonconformist the true Tory could have no good word. Of Richard Baxter's works Johnson said: "Read any of them; they are all good." He praised Grove's essays, and he added to his publisher's list of poets the name of Isaac Watts, a convert to dissent, "whom every Christian Church would rejoice to have adopted." The true Tory kept Fridays and all the days of Passion Week as fasts. Johnson regularly dined out, indeed the club met, on Fridays. In one Passion Week he dined out twice, and each time with a bishop. Clearly there was no little of the Whig in him crossing the pure Tory strain.

There remains the question of Johnson's civil politics. If here he seemed to be a Tory, it was because he had a profound disbelief in the power of Government for good or evil. Witness the couplet which he added to Goldsmith's "Traveller":

> "How small of all that human hearts endure
> That part which laws or kings can cause or cure."

He always harped on the same theme in prose. "I would not give half a guinea to live under one form of Government rather than another. It is of no moment to the happiness of an individual. Sir, the danger of the abuse of power is nothing to a private man. What Frenchman is prevented from passing his life as he pleases?" This did not mean that he had no patriotic spirit. Against the foreigner he would have shouldered a pike as readily as Socrates. The independence of the nation he valued as highly as his own personal freedom. Of this he was, as Dr. Maxwell wrote, extremely jealous. He was against certain forms of Government, but he had no fear of them. He was ready to assert that under an absolute prince men are governed by chance. There is no security for good government. But he held that the disease involved its remedy. "If a sovereign oppresses his people to a great degree, they will rise and cut off his head." It is needless to quote what Lord Auchinleck said to Johnson of Cromwell's great achievement. Of that Johnson always thought with indignation, but the Revolution he admitted to have been necessary. It is true that the Revolution found supporters among Tories of the type of Lord Nottingham, but it was a sad declension from Tory principles. Johnson said that it broke our Constitution. It broke his Toryism as well. But for that he would hardly have described a courtier as one whose business it is to watch the looks of a being as weak and foolish as himself. He retained a sentimental affection for the Stuarts, but it would stand no test. He looked at the Jacobites with a Whig's eyes. When it was observed that the Highlanders in 1745 made surprising efforts, considering their immense wants and disadvantages, "Yes, sir," said he, "their wants were immense; but you have not mentioned the greatest of them all, the want of law." So in theory he was all for a Tory Government, in practice he preferred to see the Whigs in power. Much as he hated, and rightly hated, government by corruption, he praised Sir Robert Walpole as a fixed star. When, forty years after Walpole's fall, Lord North was driven from power,

Johnson solemnly thanked God. The instinct was right that made Lord North no friend to the author of the "False Alarm." What wonder that, with this general disregard for political parties, Johnson had no delight in talking of public affairs? What wonder that he was intimate with earnest Whigs? His oldest friend was Taylor, a Whig parson. The man he admired most was perhaps Burke; the physician to whom he entrusted his dying frame was Brocklesby, and Brocklesby's admiration for Burke's politics transferred thousands of pounds from his own purse to his friend's. In this spirit Johnson dictated to Boswell his views on parties. "A wise Tory and a wise Whig, I believe, will agree. Their principles are the same, though their modes of thinking are different. A high Tory makes government unintelligible; it is lost in the clouds. A violent Whig makes it impracticable; he is for allowing so much liberty to every man, that there is not power enough to govern any man." What is there here of Macaulay's bigoted Tory? In fact, Macaulay had no appreciation of irony, and the lack of this faculty made him ascribe bigotry to Johnson as it made him turn Horace Walpole into a gentleman usher.

There was, however, one matter in which Johnson showed such a monstrous perversity that even the faithful Boswell fell away from him. He could not away with the claims of America. "Taxation no Tyranny" is indeed a lamentable pamphlet, but it is not

Toryism. A sentence here and there undoubtedly smacks of the Tory. "An English individual," he wrote, "may by the supreme authority be deprived of liberty, and a colony divested of its powers, for reasons of which that authority is the only judge." Yet he admitted that the sovereign power is not infallible, for it may do wrong. The remedy is rebellion. He argued that England had a legal right to tax America, and the Whigs, except Chatham, held the same view. He did not see that it was a legal right which ought not to be enforced and against which America might and must rebel. In fact, much of the argument of his pamphlet is not so much wrong in itself as hopelessly beside the mark; and it is beside the mark not because Johnson was a Tory, but just because he was indifferent to the forms of Government. Thus he was distracted from the main issue to subsidiary points, and at such a crisis subsidiary points could have no weight. The British army had protected America against the French; why should America not help to pay for the British army? If America were free, her own Government would tax her above any possible taxation from England; was it not wicked to refuse to pay? Would the mere sound of freedom make the Bostonians abandon their homes? If so, let no man thereafter doubt the story of the Pied Piper. Clearly, nothing would have made Johnson believe Burke's Philadelphian correspondent, who wrote that the plain farmer and even the plain Quaker was become a soldier, "a man of iron, armed at all points, despising danger, and praying for another frolic with Howe and his redcoats." His patriotism might have gained force upon the field of Marathon, but he could not understand a patriot that wielded the sword against a Government of his own race. If blindness to the warnings of history is synonymous with Toryism, then undoubtedly Johnson was a Tory. Indeed, his state of mind made him as blind as Dean Tucker of Gloucester, who in ungrammatical frenzy had screamed to Necker that the future grandeur of America was "one of the idlest and most visionary notions that ever was conceived even by writers of romance." The Whigs were perhaps right in doubting the political prescience of the parson. Johnson's name is great enough to have lived down his political pamphlets. Tucker's name and pamphlets are alike forgotten.

Johnson, then, was no party politician. In a small Northamptonshire church there is an epitaph to a member of the house of Fitzroy, which may be taken either as an antithesis or as a climax. "Through life a consistent Liberal, he died in the Lord." There is no political term that we can substitute for Liberal to make the epitaph serve as Johnson's. We *can* say that his life was like his death, and that his death was as the Northamptonshire squire's.

DR. JOHNSON'S ASSOCIATIONS WITH THE LAW, THE LAWYERS, AND LEGAL HAUNTS

A Paper read before the Johnson Club

BY

ARTHUR H. SPOKES
Recorder of Reading

JOHNSON'S LODGINGS IN THE TEMPLE.

[To face p. 203]

Dr. Johnson's Associations with the Law, the Lawyers, and Legal Haunts

DR. JOHNSON had throughout his life a predilection for the law. When some one in his company was making the usual complaints against the law, Johnson interrupted him, "Let us hear, sir, no general abuse— the law is the last result of human wisdom acting upon human experience for the benefit of the public."

At various periods of his life he meditated applying himself to the practice of the law. In 1738 he made efforts to gain admittance to the ancient legal fraternity of Doctors' Commons; but he found that he was disqualified by the lack of a University degree. In 1765, just after he had received the diploma of LL.D. from the University of Dublin, he again thought of entering the legal profession; for we find amongst his Meditations a "Prayer before the Study of the Law," in which he prays that he may be qualified "to direct the doubtful and instruct the ignorant; to prevent wrongs and terminate contentions." In 1778 he said to Boswell, "I ought to have been a lawyer," and a discussion ensued as to whether he had done more good to the world by compiling the Dictionary than by becoming Lord Chancellor. On another occasion—upon the death of Lord Lichfield—Sir William Scott lamented to Johnson that he had not followed the profession, and suggested that he might have become Lord Chancellor and taken the now extinct title of Lord Lichfield. Johnson took the suggestion quite seriously, and said with some bitterness, "Why will you vex me by suggesting this when it is too late?"

But although he never engaged in systematic study of the law, his views on legal questions were singularly profound and forcible. We find him talking with great knowledge and clearness of vision on the law of entails, the registration of deeds, the defects of case law, and a multitude of abstruse legal topics. He was always ready to analyse and discuss a legal point just as eagerly as any other point. Whenever Boswell had a brief he applied to Johnson to compose the argument. Thus we find this untrained layman writing an elaborate disquisition (occupying four closely printed pages) on the intricate subject of "vicious intromission" by an administrator, and controverting the learned Lord Kames upon this obscure point of Scotch law. Boswell put before him his pet case of the ejected schoolmaster with merciless iteration, until Johnson had discussed it from every imaginable point of view. An exhaustive argument on "verbal injuries" was extracted from him in the curious libel action brought by a Scotch doctor, who complained that in the translation of a Latin charter he was called a "doctor of medicine" instead of a "physician." In an argument for another action of libel (brought by the Society of Procurators at Edinburgh) he drew an ingenious distinction between writing *animo injurandi* and writing *animo irritandi*— a distinction which I regret to say the Courts have not adopted. If Johnson had had his way a libel which irritates but does not injure would not be actionable. He also maintained in an argument with Mr. Murray, Solicitor-General for Scotland, that there ought to be no prosecutions for libels on the dead, saying, "If a man could say nothing against a character but what he can prove history could not be written." I must not omit to mention a pleading of a very different kind—he wrote the speech which the unfortunate Doctor Dodd addressed to the Recorder of London in the awful moment before sentence of death was passed upon him. In another famous trial at the Old Bailey, Johnson—in company with Burke and Garrick—was a witness to character for his friend Baretti. We are told that "he gave his evidence in a slow, deliberate, and distinct manner, which was uncommonly impressive."

And I cannot help mentioning (though it is hardly

pertinent to the subject of this paper) Dr. Johnson's appearance in the novel character of an "executor." Never having had much property of his own, he was very proud of administering the estate of another. On the day of the auction at Thrale's brewery he bustled about with an inkhorn and a pen in his buttonhole, saying, "We are not here to sell a parcel of boilers and vats, but the potentiality of growing rich beyond the dreams of avarice."

We are told in the Johnsoniana that "he thought very favourably of the profession in general, and said the sages of the law for a long series backward had been friends to religion." But after reading his remarks in conversation I do not think he had much sympathy with the practising lawyers of his time. He looked upon them in general as machines wound up by precedents and set going by fees. He lamented their neglect of principles and their slavish adherence to cases, and he wished that we had here—as on the continent—lawyers who should write and lecture without being narrowed by legal practice. Of attorneys he seems to have had a bad opinion—in "London" we find him saying—"And there the fell attorney prowls for prey." On one occasion when a gentleman had quitted the company and there was much inquiry as to who he might be, Johnson at length said "he did not care to speak ill of any man behind his back, but he believed the gentleman was an attorney."

DR. JOHNSON'S ASSOCIATIONS

It is curious that Johnson never even met Lord Mansfield. Although the illustrious Chief Justice expressed great respect for him, Johnson never could be persuaded to go to the Sunday evening receptions at the noble mansion in Bloomsbury Square. In fact, he thought very little of the intellectual character of "silver-tongued Murray," and said with a kind of proud contempt, "Sir, I never was in Lord Mansfield's company." And referring to him on another occasion, he said, "It is wonderful with how little real superiority of mind men can make an eminent figure in public life." Concerning another law lord who took a fancy to associate with the wits of London he said, "This man has now been ten years about town and has made nothing of it. I never heard anything from him in company that was at all striking; and depend upon it, sir, it is when you come close to a man in conversation that you discover what his real abilities are. To make a speech in a public assembly is a knack. Now, I honour Thurlow, sir; Thurlow is a fine fellow—he fairly puts his mind to yours."

On another occasion he said, "I would prepare myself for no man in England but Lord Thurlow. When I am to meet him I should wish to know a day before." Thurlow reciprocated this affectionate respect. When Johnson was ill and 75 years old, Thurlow did his best to obtain from the Government the means to enable Johnson to spend the winter in

Italy; and failing in this endeavour, he offered to advance the necessary sum himself on a nominal mortgage of the pension.

Wedderburn (afterwards Lord Loughborough) was another brilliant lawyer amongst Johnson's friends. He was the first person who mentioned the matter of the pension to Lord Bute. And Johnson defended Wedderburn against old Mr. Sheridan's complaint that the successful lawyer was ungrateful for Sheridan's assistance in teaching him elocution in his early days.

Johnson was often in the company of William Scott—the elder brother of Lord Eldon. He afterwards became Lord Stowell, and was the greatest judge who has ever presided over our Admiralty Court. Johnson was present at a dinner at his chambers in the Temple on April 10, 1778, which was followed by one of the most interesting of the many conversations in which Johnson took part.

Johnson was introduced to Erskine in 1772, long before he became the eloquent advocate and accomplished judge, and this acquaintance lasted many years. He must also have known Blackstone, who lived underneath Goldsmith in Brick Court.

But it is of course among the lesser lights of the profession that we find the intimate friends of his every-day life. He once told Boswell, "I learnt what I know of law chiefly from Mr. Ballow, a very able man. I learnt some too from Chambers." All I can find out about Ballow is that he wrote an excellent

"Treatise of Equity," and was a great Greek scholar. Chambers lived close to Johnson in the Temple for many years, and they had many midnight talks and convivial suppers together. He afterwards became an Indian Judge, and when he went to India was the bearer of a respectful letter from Johnson to the then Governor of Bengal—Warren Hastings.

Dr. Maxwell, the reader of the Temple, tells us that Johnson very much loved Arthur Murphy. In 1762, Murphy—then a briefless barrister—came as Wedderburn's messenger to offer Johnson the pension. He found Johnson in Inner Temple Lane, which he describes as "an abode of wretchedness." Next day Johnson and Murphy had a convivial dinner at the "Mitre," after which Johnson finally consented to accept the pension. Arthur Murphy took to writing plays, and Johnson said of him as a dramatic writer, "At present I doubt whether we have anything superior to Arthur."

In the other branch of the profession Sir John Hawkins is the only friend I can trace. He it was who, at the Club, begged to be excused his share of the reckoning, on the ground that he took no supper. Johnson not unnaturally thought him "a very unclubable man," and "rather penurious and somewhat mean." He said, "We all admitted his plea publicly for the gratification of scorning him privately."

His advice to one who wished to succeed at the bar and yet to enjoy life deserves to be quoted. "When not actually employed you may see your friends as much as you do now. You may dine at a club every day and sup with one of the members every night. But you must take care to attend constantly at Westminster Hall—both to mind your business and to show that you want to have business. And you must not be too often seen at public places, that competitors may not have it to say, 'He is always at the playhouse, or Ranelagh, and never to be found at his chambers.' And, sir, there must be a kind of solemnity about a professional man." The hackneyed question as to whether an advocate might support a cause which he knows to be bad he disposed of by saying, " Sir, you do not know a cause to be good or bad till the Judge determines it."

As to advocacy his advice was, "You must say the same thing over and over again in different words. If you say it but once they miss it in a moment of inattention. It is unjust, sir, to censure lawyers for multiplying words—it is often *necessary* to multiply words."

Johnson lived in legal haunts for thirty-six years. The Inns of Court of those days were very different from the present, and very different, too, from the legal University of the reign of Henry VI., which we are told was crowded with students from all parts of the country. The " Law List " for 1770 reveals the astonishing fact that there were less than 300 men even nominally at the bar. Yet the buildings covered almost as much ground as they do now. It is obvious, therefore, that the ample space of the Temples and Lincoln's Inn must have been largely used for other than legal purposes. When a member of an Inn married in those days he brought his wife to live there, and we may imagine that the lady enjoyed the society of her husband's friends, and the husband did not feel that marriage means his banishment from those informal and unconstrained occasions of mirth which the members of this club so often enjoy. When a man came up to town to seek a living by literature, he often settled down in an Inn of Court or Chancery. There he wrote his poems and his plays; there he was visited by printers' devils and dunned by creditors; there he gave the joyous suppers we read of; and there often he died in poverty, blessed only by his laundress's alcoholic tears. Ford, Marston, and Beaumont, Raleigh, Selden and Clarendon, Wycherley and Congreve, had all sojourned in the Temple.

It was natural that Johnson, too, should gravitate to this sociable and unconventional quarter. He did not care for fashionable society or set parties; he loved a good long talk in a plain man's room, where he could dress and behave as he liked. In 1748 he came to Gough Square, and from that time till his death he lived in the legal quarter. After ten years in Gough Square he removed—apparently through poverty—to Staple Inn, which is even now the cheapest place a man may live in. In the same year, 1759, we find him in Gray's Inn—the house he lived in being probably in Field Court. All we know about it is that it was a "cheap lodging."

About 1759 or 1760 he removed to Inner Temple Lane, and it is there that we have the most frequent glimpses of him. The house was the first on the right hand as you enter the Temple from Fleet Street. It was of quaint red brick—built in the fifteenth year of James I. It is gone now—pulled down some twenty years ago—and replaced by a hideous grey structure known as Dr. Johnson's Buildings. Ozias Humphrey, the painter, thus describes these chambers, "We passed through three very dirty rooms to a little one, that looked like an old counting-house—where this great man was sat at breakfast." Arthur Murphy speaks of him as living here in poverty, total idleness, and the pride of literature. Mr. Fitzherbert desiring one morning to write a letter there found the chambers destitute of pen, ink, and paper. Madame de Bouffler (a French bluestocking of doubtful reputation) came to see him at these chambers; and we are told that after he had bidden her adieu, Johnson was seized with a sudden fit of gallantry, that he rushed downstairs into Inner Temple Lane with a noise like thunder, seized the lady's hand, and conducted her to her coach. It was here that Beauclerk and Langton knocked him up at three in the morning for that riotous frisk in Covent Garden, followed by a day spent in dissipation and the drinking of "bishop."

The rooms in the Temple where Johnson spent the most cheerful evenings were those of Oliver Goldsmith and Robert Chambers. Early in 1764 Goldsmith removed from Wine Office Court to chambers on the library staircase of the Middle Temple, and so poor was he that he had to share them with the butler of the Society—one Jeffs. When Johnson paid his first visit there, Goldsmith began with apologies for living in this menial abode, "I shall soon be in better chambers than these, sir." Johnson checked him with manly philosophy, "Nay, sir, never mind that, *Nil te quaesiveris extra.*" But poor Goldsmith could not refrain from seeking externals. On receiving some £500 for the "Good Natured Man" in 1768 he spent nearly all of it in purchasing a handsome set of chambers in Brick Court and in furnishing them luxuriously. These chambers (second floor, right hand side of No. 2) still stand, and they are the most abiding and unaltered memorial of Dr. Johnson. There has been no material change in them since his time. The floor is the one he trod—the panels that we see echoed with his laughter. It was here that he joined in those uproarious parties which so disturbed the peace of Sir W. Blackstone, who sat writing his commentaries on the floor below with a bottle of port before him.

It was in the rooms of Robert Chambers, in Farrar's Buildings, that he passed the evening before indulging in that famous fit of laughter at the Temple gateway which, being totally unaccounted for by any adequate cause, made such an impression on his awestricken friends, and has been a mystery to succeeding generations. Hours had been passed in small jokes about a will which Chambers had drawn for one of the company—whom Johnson persisted in addressing as "testator." On leaving the party, Johnson could not stop his merriment, but continued it all the way till he got without the Temple gate. He then laid hold of one of the posts by the footway and sent forth peals of laughter, so loud that they were heard from Temple Bar to the Fleet Ditch.

When Johnson removed from the Temple, in 1765, it was only to Johnson's Court—already named after another Johnson now unknown, probably a speculative builder—on the other side of Fleet Street; and there and at Bolt Court he lived until his death. During these nineteen years he continued the associations and acquaintances begun in Gough Square and the Temple. He was still in the legal quarter—still in the centre of all that was most attractive in London. Dinners continued at the "Mitre," the "Rainbow," and the "Cock." Suppers and uproarious mirth still went on in the chambers hard by; and many a night the Temple porter let out of the ancient gateway the rolling figure whose peals of laughter in Fleet Street were the wonder of his contemporaries.

We, living in this big London, may well envy that compact and joyous community, most of whom lived

DR. JOHNSON'S ASSOCIATIONS

but a few minutes' walk from each other. North of Oxford Street there were then very few houses, and south of the river we are told that Johnson saw the green hills of Surrey from the Temple gardens. Within the limits of Gerrard Street, on the west, and the Fleet Ditch, on the east, was gathered all that a literary man of the eighteenth century cared for. Now, if a modern Johnsonian wants to visit his brethren, he must travel from Epping Forest to Bedford Park, and from Highgate to Dulwich.

However, it is no use sighing over the past. If we cannot meet as often as Johnson and his friends did, let us concentrate into our rare gatherings as much good fellowship as they spread over the whole year. Let us imitate their warm sympathy, their reasonable merriment, and, above all, their love of real conversation —which Johnson defines as "fairly putting his mind to yours."

DR. JOHNSON AS A CORRESPONDENT

Read at a Meeting of the Johnson Club

by

ALFRED WEST

THE ROOM IN THE "CHESHIRE CHEESE" WHERE THE JOHNSON CLUB USUALLY MEETS.

Dr. Johnson as a Correspondent

Many of those who are present this evening visited the Westminster Town Hall last month, on charitable thoughts intent, to hear the lecture on Dr. Johnson, delivered by our late Prior, Augustine Birrell. These philanthropists learnt the luxury of doing good, in a sense not contemplated by the poet. For our friend's discourse reflected credit on the rank-and-file of the club to which it is our pride to belong. I am in some doubt whether I correctly grasped the central idea which the lecture exemplified and developed, for there were proud patrician dames in my neighbourhood, who gossipped and giggled from first to last, with a graceful disregard of other people's convenience peculiar to the British aristocracy. But I think that the root of the matter was the transmission of personality, and the marks by which we trace it. "Personality," like Mesopotamia, is a blessed word, full of comfort for the hungry soul. And "transmission of personality" has about it a *soupçon* of metaphysical subtlety which bestows upon a subject the flavour, not only of respectability, but of distinction. To show in detail how Johnson's correspondence indicates those traits of character with which Boswell's "Life" has made us familiar, would be, for any ardent Johnsonian, a labour of love. But he would probably find himself largely forestalled by that prince of editors, Dr. Birkbeck Hill, or, if gleanings remained, the exercise of gathering them in would be too severely academical for a festive occasion. The venerable Paley performed the like pious office when he traced coincidences between the epistles of St. Paul and the narrative in the Acts of the Apostles. But the "Horæ Paulinæ," admirable monument of industrious research though it is, lacks the qualities which tend to foster after-dinner merriment. "We meet at table," as Johnson told Boswell, "to eat and drink together and to promote kindness, and, sir, this is better done when there is no solid conversation."[1] I propose, therefore, to offer only a few discursive remarks, mainly trivial and often incoherent.

Let us hear the great man himself on letters as an index to character. The following extract from a letter to Mrs. Thrale, written in 1777, contains a curious blend of the somewhat pompous philosophical style of the "Rambler," with its caricature, in a spirit of playfulness and pleasantry, by its creator.

"In a man's letters, you know, madam, his soul lies

Boswell, "Life of Johnson," vol. iii. p. 57, Clarendon Press edition.

naked; his letters are only the mirror of his breast; whatever passes within him is shown undisguised in its natural process: nothing is inverted, nothing distorted; you see systems in their elements; you discover actions in their motives.

"Of this great truth, sounded by the knowing to the ignorant, and so echoed by the ignorant to the knowing, what evidence have you now before you? Is not my soul laid open in these veracious pages? Do not you see me reduced to my first principles? This is the pleasure of corresponding with a friend, where doubt and distrust have no place, and everything is said as it is thought. The original idea is laid down in its simple purity, and all the supervenient conceptions are spread over it *stratum super stratum*, as they happen to be formed. . . . I know, dearest lady, that in the perusal of this, such is the consanguinity of our intellects, you will be touched as I am touched. I have indeed concealed nothing from you, nor do I expect ever to repent of having thus opened my heart."[1]

Nevertheless, the inquirer who searches for personality in letters and diaries must draw his conclusions with cautious reserve. Johnson was a believer in keeping a journal, though he never persevered in keeping one himself. "The great thing to be recorded," he said, "is the state of your own mind."[2] Unfortunately, as George Eliot has remarked, people

[1] Johnson's "Letters," vol. ii. p. 52, Clarendon Press edition.
[2] Vol. ii. p. 217.

find it a great deal easier to say a number of fine and striking things about their state of mind than to tell us exactly what their state of mind is.

Still, the truth leaks out occasionally in a diary, as it does in an affidavit, and letters are pretty sure to blab. Yet a wise man feels that, when produced as witnesses to character, they need corroboration. For as Johnson admits in his "Life of Pope," "There is indeed no transaction which offers stronger temptations to fallacy and sophistication than epistolary intercourse." Pope's "epistolary intercourse" is certainly better calculated than most men's to bring home to one's mind the truth of this remark. I suppose we should none of us judge a criminal, or, for that matter, a diplomatist, by his correspondence. In these days, when to read and write comes by nature, a convict awaiting execution, after a fortnight's acquaintance with the prison chaplain, usually addresses a letter to his friends or to the public, abounding in beautiful thoughts and fragrant with the spirit of holiness. But we know very well that the voice is the voice of the divine, though the hand is the hand of the convict. The case is one, not of transmitted, but of transmuted personality.

Buffon's aphorism declares, indeed, that "the style is the man himself"; but then another aphorism, not more mendacious, maintains that "language was given us in order that we might conceal our thoughts." Buffon ignored the possibility of successfully simulating the style of somebody else. If it were true that the style reveals the man, we may feel quite sure that many a copious writer would think twice before he ran the risk of exposing his personality in all its naked indecency on paper.

Then, again, in using letters as a test of personality, we must remember the Autocrat's doctrine that, when two people take part in a dialogue, six personalities are brought into the field; and the same thing occurs in correspondence. Thus, when John and Thomas exchange communications, we have not one John, but three Johns; not one Thomas, but three Thomases. There is (1) the real John, known only to his Maker; (2) John's ideal John, never the real one, and often very unlike him; (3) Thomas's ideal John, never the real John, nor John's John, but often very unlike both.[1] And, similarly, there are three Thomases.

Now, Silly Billy satisfied the Bishop of Exeter that idiots were suitable subjects for confirmation when he showed his grasp of the doctrine of the Trinity.

"What does Silly Billy see?"

"Three in One and One in Three."

Nevertheless, the problem of discriminating between the real and the ideal personalities in the case of John or Thomas presents some difficulty.

Johnson's letters are in various styles, all of them excellent of their kind. There is the letter in which he gave Lord Chesterfield a piece of his mind, "one

[1] "Autocrat of the Breakfast Table," vol. i. p. 75.

of those knock-down blows," as Mr. Leslie Stephen says, "to which no answer is possible, and upon which comment is superfluous." Quotation is also superfluous. A certain amount of elaboration was due to the peer. A few lines sufficed to give Macpherson his quietus.

"Mr. Macpherson,—I received your foolish and impudent letter. Any violence offered me I shall do my best to repel; and what I cannot do for myself the law shall do for me. I hope I shall never be deterred from detecting what I think a cheat by the menaces of a ruffian."

This couldn't be better. The concluding sentence, "You may print this if you will," is courteous, but the permission was unnecessary.

The letters to Mrs. Thrale are delightful—spontaneous, sportive, sometimes almost skittish, yet they never remind us of the painful gambols of an elephant. Johnson understood "the great epistolick art." "Some," he says, "when they write to their friends, are all affection; some are wise and sententious; some strain their powers for efforts of gaiety; some write news, and some write secrets. But to make a letter without affection, without wisdom, without gaiety, without news, and without a secret, is, doubtless, the great epistolick art." [1]

[1] "Letters," vol. ii. p. 52.

DR. JOHNSON AS A CORRESPONDENT

To obtain a just impression of Johnson's letters to Mrs. Thrale one must read them in the lump. An isolated specimen gives an inadequate and misleading representation of the correspondence as a whole. It resembles the solitary brick which was carried round by the simpleton in the old Greek jape to indicate the architectural style of the building to which it belonged. I therefore forbear to quote.

Alas! that after nearly twenty years of friendly intercourse, the same kind hand should have penned the following outburst of fury :—

"MADAM,—If I interpret your letter right, you are ignominiously married. If it is yet undone, let us once more talk together. If you have abandoned your children and your religion, God forgive your wickedness. If you have forfeited your fame and your country, may your folly do no further mischief. If the last act is yet to do, I who have loved you, esteemed you, reverenced you, and served you, I who long thought you the first of womankind, entreat that, before your fate is irrevocable, I may once more see you. I was, I once was,

"Madam, most truly yours,
"SAM. JOHNSON.

"*July* 2, 1784.

"I will come down if you will permit it."

"How sad, and bad, and mad it was!" and how

futile! For of course Mrs. Thrale married her foreign fiddler; and it is pleasant to add that she lived happily enough with him ever afterwards.

Johnson's friends must have been frequently amused, and occasionally bored, by the pertinacity with which he inquired after their symptoms and prescribed for their ailments. To Mrs. Thrale he writes: "It appears to me that Mr. Thrale's disorder, whether grumous or serous, must be cured by bleeding, and I would not have him begin a course of exercise without considerable evacuation. To increase the force of the blood, unless it be first diluted and attenuated, may be dangerous. But the case," he modestly adds, "is too important for my theory."[1]

In other letters to the same lady he discusses diacodium,[2] vesicatories, and a diffusion of cantharides;[3] declares himself "of the chymical sect which holds phlebotomy in abhorrence,"[4] yet admits that "gentle purges and slight phlebotomies are not his favourites; they are pop-gun batteries, which lose time and effect nothing." Thrale must "trust chiefly to vigorous and stimulating cathartics."[5]

"Had anything disturbed you?" he asks the well-beneficed clergyman, Dr. Taylor. "I have but two rules for you—keep your body open, and your mind quiet."[6]

[1] Vol. ii. p. 103.   [2] Ibid. p. 253.   [3] Ibid. p. 304.
[4] Ibid. p. 253.   [5] Ibid. p. 198.   [6] Ibid. p. 277.

Admirable advice for us all! Counsels of perfection, however.

"My sweet Angel," he writes to the excellent Miss Boothby, "My sweet Angel... Give me leave, who have thought much on medicine, to propose to you an easy, and I think a very probable remedy for indigestion and lubricity of the bowels. Dr. Lawrence has told me your case. Take an ounce of dried orange-peel, finely powdered, divide it into scruples, and take one scruple at a time... This is a medicine not disgusting, not costly, easily tried, and if not found useful, easily left off. I would not have you offer it to the Doctor as mine. Physicians do not love intruders. Yet do not take it without his leave. But do not be easily put off, for it is in my opinion very likely to help you, and not likely to do you harm."[1]

Thus it is that to Miss Boothby's constitutional infirmity the world owes the solution of a problem which baffled Boswell's curiosity.

"Pray, sir, what do you do with them?" asked Boswell, pointing to the peels of squeezed oranges, pocketed the night before at the Club. "You scrape them, it seems, very neatly, and what next?" "Let them dry, sir." "And what next?" "Nay, sir, you shall know their fate no further." "Then the work must be left in the dark. It must be said, he scraped them, and let them dry, but what he did with them he never could be prevailed upon to tell." "Nay, sir,

[1] Vol. i. p. 49.

you should say it more emphatically—he could not be prevailed upon, even by his dearest friends, to tell."[1]

Johnson's letters to his mother express in the simplest language the profoundest reverence and love. To read the three letters which he addressed to her in the course of five days during the last week of her life produces on the mind the elevating effects of a religious exercise. At a convivial gathering they are out of keeping, and I pass them by.

There are some men's letters which we read because we are interested in the personality of the writer; others which we read for their literary charm, though the personality is nought; others again which attract us for both reasons. In the last category, without any hesitation, I place Johnson's. Private letters, written by a man for whose personality we don't care two straws, in a style devoid of conspicuous literary merit, should be rigorously shielded from the public gaze for at least a century.

Take Swift's letters, which the gentle Cowper thought "the best that could be written," till he read Gray's, and confessed that he "liked Gray's better." What is the quality which makes an octavo volume of daily letters addressed to Stella readable at the present day? Here is a sample, dated January 16, 1711.

"My service to Mrs. Stode and Walls. Has she a boy or a girl? A girl, hmm! and died in a week,

[1] "Life," ii. 330.

him-m-m! And was poor Stella forced to stand for godmother? Let me know how accounts stand, that you may have your money betimes. There's four months for my lodging; that must be thought on too. And zoo go dine with Manley, and lose your money, doo extravagant sluttikin? But don't fret. It will be just three weeks when I have the next letter, that is, to-morrow. Farewell, dearest beloved M. D., and love poor, poor Presto, who has not had one happy day since he left you, as hope to be saved."

Similar passages from the defendant's correspondence, read in court by Lockwood, Q.C., in a modern breach of promise action, would be punctuated with roars of laughter. Here we have, as Matthew Arnold would say, not *simplicité* but *simplesse*—sheer drivel, in short—interesting, however, because we are already interested in the personality of the writer; interesting, because it shows the black-browed Irish vicar in a new light—shows that the domineering genius, before whom Ministers of State cringed and trembled, had depths of tenderness which prompted him to prattle fondly and foolishly of an evening to the "dear girls at Laracor."

Take, by way of contrast, Horace Walpole's letters. If I were restricted to one man's correspondence, Walpole would be the man of my choice. Macaulay describes him as "the most eccentric, the most artificial, the most fastidious, the most capricious of men . . . a bundle of inconsistent whims and affectations, ... a Diogenes who was a gentleman-usher at heart, ... a character combining the vanity, the jealousy, the irritability of a man of letters with the affected superciliousness and apathy of a man of *ton*, ..." and so on, in the style we know so well. Yet Macaulay admits "the charm, the irresistible charm of Walpole's writings." "No man," he says, " who has written so much is so seldom tiresome. In his books there are scarcely any of those passages which, in our school-days, we used to call *skip*." With Walpole the personality counts for nothing. The style is all in all.

In turning from Walpole's letters to those of his travelling companion, Gray, we pass from the world of fashion to the "cloistered seclusion of college." In Gray's letters we see the virtues and the weaknesses of the man, "his purity, his gentleness, his love of books, and his almost effeminate shrinking, not only from active life, but also from social intercourse with mankind or womankind." Perhaps it was owing to this last feature in his character that Johnson found Gray "a dull fellow,—dull in company, dull in his closet, dull everywhere." A curious criticism, but it deserves recording. Alongside of Gray's correspondence we may place Cowper's—perhaps "the purest and most perfect specimens of familiar letters in our language."

Of letters which appeal to us by reason both of their own merit as compositions and of the personality of the writer, Byron's would be hard to beat. This opinion stamps me, I fear, as a fossil, for has not Professor Saintsbury pronounced that Byron is only a poet of the second class, and not high in that?

In the memoir of the poet Cowley, written by his friend Dr. Sprat—"the florid Sprat"—and addressed to another friend, whom the elegant solecism of to-day would describe as "mutual," a passage occurs which is worthy of consideration at the present time. Dr. Sprat says:—

"There was one kind of prose wherein Mr. Cowley was excellent, and that is his letters to his private friends. In those he always expressed the native tenderness and innocent gaiety of his mind. I think, sir, you and I have the greatest collection of this sort. But I know you agree with me that nothing of this sort should be published. . . . The truth is, the letters that pass between particular friends, if they are written as they ought to be, can scarce ever be fit to see the light. They should not consist of fulsome compliments, or tedious politics, or elaborate elegancies, or general fancies; but they should have a native clearness and shortness, a domestical plainness, and a peculiar kind of familiarity, which can affect the humour only of those for whom they were intended. The very same passages which make writings of this nature delightful among friends, will lose all manner of taste when they come to be read by those that are indifferent. In such letters, the souls of men should appear undressed; and in that negligent habit they may be fit to be seen by one or two in a chamber, but not to go abroad in the street."

So far Dr. Sprat. Let us respect the delicacy of his sentiment, even though we lament the application of his reasoning. The very perfection of the letters forms the ground on which he withholds them from publication.

Now let us listen for a moment to the editor of Matthew Arnold's correspondence, if indeed two volumes can be said to be edited at all when they are pitchforked upon the public without an analysis of their contents or an index, and proper names are spelt with a liberal disregard of orthography.

The preface tells us that the letters are printed because it was thought that "such a selection might reveal aspects of his character—his tenderness and playfulness and filial affection—which could be only imperfectly apprehended through the more formal medium of his published works. . . . The letters are essentially familiar and domestic, and were evidently written without a thought that they would ever be read beyond the circle of his family."

These letters should have been kept back for fifty years. By that time there might be no demand for their publication at all. To publish them now is an outrage. I suppose that each of us numbers on his list of friends one or two correspondents whose hand-writing, outside the envelope, affords a sure and certain hope that something good will be found within. Happy the man who numbers several such! But what security in writing will they feel, if "the barriers of reserve are to fall before the cupidity of booksellers, the vanity of editors, or the vicious curiosity of the reading public?"

Our interest was not in Matthew Arnold the man, but in his artistic handiwork, his exquisite literary fiddling, which had delighted us for nearly thirty years. The man was a bundle of quaint prejudices—mainly against Dissenters, for wanting to marry their deceased wives' sisters—prejudices not particularly creditable in a thinker who wished to be taken seriously. The artist, in his own style, was supreme. But this supreme literary fiddling is entirely absent from the letters, most of which might have been written by "many men, many women, and many children." As Literature they are dull, and as Dogma they are often deplorable.

Half a century hence, I daresay there will be people who will read every scrap of correspondence that Carlyle wrote, just as there are people now who read every scrap of correspondence that Johnson wrote. But Matthew Arnold was not Carlyle. Who is the better for hearing that his editor asked Matthew Arnold to dinner, and that Matthew Arnold declined the invitation? Is it not cruel to publish to the English-speaking world a note of this sort?

"*April* 28, 1887.

"My dear George,—I am going to Aston Clinton on Wednesday 4th, and must return to my forsaken ones here on Friday 6th.

"Besides, —— would certainly say, if I dined with you again, that it was because not a bone was left in the cupboard in Grub Street.

"We have designs on you for a Sunday here, but Mrs. Arnold will write.

"Ever yours affectionately,

"M. A."

A nice little note for Matthew Arnold to write: but what are we say of "My dear George," who converts it into a catholic epistle, to be known and read of all men? The only point of human interest is a mild curiosity as to Blank's identity, and Blank's identity is not divulged. Let us be grateful, however, for the faintest indications of a decorous reserve.

What concern is it of ours to know that Matthew Arnold was an affectionate son, a good husband, a kind father? Do we pry into the domestic interior of our butcher, or simulate an interest in "the tenderness and playfulness and filial affection" of our milkman?

Year after year we may have enjoyed the erudition of Smith in the *Spectator*, the persiflage of Brown in the *News*, the moral earnestness of Jones in the *Chronicle*. But when Smith and Brown and Jones are finally at rest, our felicity will not be increased by the appearance of their private letters, issued for the sake of satisfying the public that Smith was strictly temperate in his habits, that Brown never bonneted a policeman, and that Jones always came home to tea.

Is there any illustrious literary man whose masterpieces of familiar correspondence are secure against this public rape? My roving fancy depicts bulky volumes tumbling in hot succession from the press—'Letters from Professor Saintsbury to "My dear Gosse," Letters from Mr. Gosse to "My dear Saintsbury," and Letters from Mr. Churton Collin about both.

In self-defence our eminent authors will have to publish their letters themselves in order to outwit their posthumous editors. Methinks I see a noble band marching on Vigo Street, every man carrying his correspondence in his hand—Mr. Grant Allen from the hilltop, blowing his trumpet in the van; Mr. William Watson raising the dithyrambic strain; Mr. Le Gallienne, a new Narcissus, enamoured of his own image; and Mr. Frederick Wedmore investing the procession with artistic grace.

Then be it ours, packing our portmanteaus with the flotsam and jetsam of the bankrupt eighteenth century—with Pope and Swift, with Goldsmith and Johnson—to shun the Serbonian bog of literary flapdoodle, and, retiring to a lodge in some vast wilderness, far from the madding crowd, with old friends, old manners, old books, and old wine, there to sing the Obsolete!

ROUND THE TOWN WITH DR. JOHNSON

A Paper read before the Johnson Club

by

GEORGE WHALE

[To face p. 2

Round the Town with Dr. Johnson[1]

WHETHER London be a pleasant place to live in, no man shall decide for another. Love of London, or dislike of London, is a question of temperament and not a matter of argument, except among those dreadful people who dispute their way through life. Many great men would not willingly have dwelt elsewhere, and of these the type, the most famous instance, has long been Dr. Johnson. None of his sayings is more quoted, in part at least, than that in which, after forty years' rough experience of London, he dispelled Boswell's doubt whether a man would not lose his zest for London if, instead of an occasional visit, he made it his residence. "Why, sir," cried Johnson, "you find no man at all intellectual who is willing to leave London. No, sir; when a man is tired of London he is tired of life, for there is in London all that life can

[1] Reprinted by kind permission from the *Gentleman's Magazine*, February, 1893.

afford. A country gentleman should bring his lady to visit London as soon as he can, that they may have agreeable topics of conversation when they are by themselves." Dr. Johnson certainly visited London early, for he was only thirty months old when his mother, as he could recollect, brought him up from Lichfield to be touched by Queen Anne for the King's evil. When about twenty-eight, Johnson commenced Londoner for life.

Thenceforward Johnson might, indeed, lodge occasionally at Greenwich, or at Hampstead, or he might visit the Thrales at Streatham, or take country holidays when his pension permitted, but he remained a Londoner, an incurable Londoner, and his love of London never left him. He mentally returned to it as he gazed on beautiful scenes. He compared his favourite Fleet Street to Tempe; and, on the visit to Greenwich Park, he readily assented to Boswell's preference for Fleet Street. On his first quitting England, which was in 1773, and for the tour in the Hebrides, we find Johnson, after two months, declaring that, "by seeing London I have seen as much life as the world can show." When Boswell thereupon rashly reminded Johnson that he had not seen Pekin, Johnson thundered out, "What is Pekin? Ten thousand Londoners would drive all the people of Pekin; they would drive them like deer." And when, four years later, Boswell, melancholy, and in Scotland, had to be consoled, it was by a letter in which Johnson said that

ROUND THE TOWN WITH JOHNSON

happiness might be had "in other places as well as London." Yet Johnson would not "debauch" Boswell's mind. He adds, "I do not blame your preference of London to other places, for it is really to be preferred if the choice is free." And, in spite of all temptations, Johnson remained a Londoner. More than once he was offered country preferment if he would take orders; but, as he told his old friend, the Rev. Dr. Maxwell, "he could not leave the improved society of the capital." He liked country holidays, but as Mrs. Thrale said, Johnson would "rather be sick in London than well in the country."

In London, then, Johnson would live. To London, in the last months of his life, he returned to die. Who shall contend against such a choice as this? Philosophers may say, as of old, that they are never less alone than when alone. Travellers may go to Pekin, or elsewhere. Poets may sing with Cowley of a small house and a large garden, or with Mr. Andrew Lang of a "house full of books and a garden of flowers," but they must at least pityingly admit that we are all happy if but well deceived, and that Johnson was happy in his London. It was not for the society of the obscure great, for he had little of it; it was not for riches, for he never over-valued them. Life, in truth, was to him more than a livelihood. He lived, like the true artist in life, for a frame of mind. It was for the freedom, for the intellectual activity, and for the social opportunities, for the things which are indeed life, that Johnson loved London.

It is fit, therefore, for us to consider what manner of place was this London of Johnson's day. We cannot now go all round the town even with Dr. Johnson. We cannot deal with all the aspects of London life then, but, whatever else we omit, we must pause to consider what London was then in size and population.

London is a word which has had in various centuries very different meanings. Once it meant the City of London as contrasted with Westminster. In our time it generally means what is called the "Metropolis," a forest of houses occupying over 75,000 acres, and containing four and a quarter millions of people. In Johnson's time it may, by an "extensive view," be taken to include London City and Westminster, the borough of Southwark, and a few then half-rural parishes, such as Hackney on the north, and Lambeth on the south, which were included in the bills of mortality. This was an area of 21,587 acres, with a population, when Johnson came up to be "touched" by Queen Anne, of a little over half a million, and, when he died, still under three-quarters of a million. This smaller London hardly grew at all in the first half of the eighteenth century; and, in the latter half, although the predecessors of the modern speculative builder tried to make the best of this world, they experienced some disappointments. The American War of Independence gave George III. and the builder a severe check, and only when the Bastille had fallen did the builder again lift up his head. But Johnson was dead then, and Johnson's London is now our concern.

It was said of old time that grass grew where Troy had been. The converse is true of London. The country is always struggling with the town, and the country has lost much ground since Johnson's day. No part of London was then situated more than a quarter of an hour's walk from fields and hedgerows. Look at the maps of London then. There is, for example, one published in the "Environs of London," by J. Roque, 1763. The mansions of Kensington and of Fitzjohn's Avenue, the closely packed dwellings, north and south, east and west, from Hornsey to Penge, and from Putney and Hammersmith to Woolwich and West Ham—where are they on this map? Here and there is seen a house or little group of houses; but, for the most part, there are only fields and commons. Chelsea, Kensington, and Paddington were rural places. The groves of St. John's Wood were unknown; and in another map, dated 1797, Hackney, Stepney, Paddington, and Chelsea are the country outskirts of the town. Until the middle of the century Rotherhithe was isolated, and until the end of the century Marylebone and St. Pancras had much less than a fourth of their present population.

Johnson's friend, General Oglethorpe, had shot woodcock in a solitude where Regent Street now stands. Johnson's acquaintance, Mrs. "Blue Stocking" Montagu, lived in Portman Square, called it the "Montpellier of England," and died aged eighty. Johnson's physician, the "virtuous and faithful Heberden," is celebrated by Cowper since he "sends the patient into purer air." Yet Heberden sent his patients to South Lambeth, because it was on the banks of a tidal river with a south-west wind "fresh from the country, and a north-east wind softened by blowing over the town." A public-house, just beyond Whitfield's Tabernacle, Tottenham Court Road, had the reputation of being the last house in London, and that reputation was, with others, only lost under the Regency. So scattered were the houses, that, from the region of Leicester Square, then Leicester Fields, the heads of the rebels of 1745 could be seen on Temple Bar. Queen's Square, Bloomsbury, was left open on the north side till after Johnson's death, that a fair country prospect might be enjoyed. Grosvenor Square was built after Boswell knew Johnson; and Portman Square was not finished till about the year of Johnson's death. It also had a fine open prospect to the north. Those suburbs to which, as Lord Rosebery says, men carry home their fish for dinner in a basket, were hardly known. Merchants generally lived in the city, as they are represented rather later in Jane Austen's novels; lawyers dwelt in or around the Inns of Court; and actors near the two theatres, Covent Garden and Drury Lane.

ROUND THE TOWN WITH JOHNSON

Yet even the London of those days did not escape the eternal flux of things. Covent Garden and Soho were ceasing to be fashionable, and Mayfair was becoming too small for the aristocracy. Up to the middle of the century they found room east of Hyde Park. Then they began to migrate to the west of it. Improvement schemes have since swept away many streets and buildings, and done much to alter London. The bad quality of the bricks, notorious so long ago as the time of Charles II., has also helped to play havoc with the buildings of Johnson's London. Fire has consumed both the House of Commons where he reported, or invented, the debates, and the Drury Lane Theatre, where, in 1749, his play "Irene" was damned whilst he "felt like the Monument."

From Charing Cross to Whitechapel, where, as Johnson told Goldsmith, there was "the greatest series of shops in the world," little remains of eighteenth - century London. His church, St. Clement Danes, "sedate and mannered elegance," as Mr. Henley calls it, St. Paul's Cathedral, part of the Bank of England, Clerkenwell Gate, the Tower, the Mansion House, and a few churches, are the chief buildings on which Johnson looked and we can look also. But who shall find the house of the Dillys, those hospitable booksellers in the Poultry who dared to entertain Johnson with Wilkes? Where now is the local habitation of the Cock Lane Ghost? And many of Johnson's own dwelling-places, his friends' houses, and his places of amusement, have gone, or cannot be identified. It is true that his residence in Gough Square stands, but where are those of Woodstock Street, or Castle Street, or Staple Inn? We shall look in vain for his chambers in the Inner Temple Lane, where, in Boswell's time, he lived in "poverty, total idleness and the pride of literature," talked as "correctly as a second edition," and received Madame de Boufflers with such a polite air. The house in Bolt Court, where the elder Disraeli left his MSS., and where Samuel Rogers knocked and ran away, was destroyed soon after Johnson's death. His taverns, which were his clubs, have also generally vanished. Some, such as the "Cheshire Cheese," and the "Cock," of Tennyson's Poem, were probably visited by him, but they have only traditional connection with Johnson's name. There were, however, others to which he undoubtedly went.

The "Pine Apple," near St. Martin's Lane, where he dined, as an abstainer, for sevenpence, and gave the waiter a penny; the "King's Head," in Ivy Lane, where one of his earliest clubs was founded, in 1748, and the "Turk's Head," Soho, where, in 1763, *The Club* was founded—these have all gone. Sadder is the loss of "The Devil Tavern," which stood between the Temple Gate and Temple Bar. It was the old tavern of Ben Jonson. There he gathered his "boys," drank seas of "canary," and received those who desired to be "sealed of the tribe of Ben."

There, too, Swift and Addison were treated to a dinner by Dr. Garth, and there Johnson, in 1751, gave that supper to Mrs. Charlotte Lennox, and nearly twenty other friends, to celebrate the birthday of the lady's first novel. At 8 p.m. they began, and at near 8 a.m. they broke up. Meanwhile, as they remembered, there had been a hot apple pie, stuck with bay leaves, and during the last three hours Johnson's face had "shone with meridian splendour," though his drink had been "only lemonade." Lemonade must have been purer then.

Since the taverns and coffee-houses in and out of Fleet Street were numerous—and Leigh Hunt is, no doubt, correct in declaring that Johnson was in every one of them—it would, perhaps, be unreasonable to expect them all still to be standing, in these days of temperance and County Councils. But the "Mitre"? Must the "Mitre" go, and the gaiety of London be eclipsed? Yes, the "Mitre," not that in Mitre Court, but the true and original "Mitre" in Fleet Street, "the orthodox high church sound of the 'Mitre,'" as Boswell said, was not safe from what Johnson, mourning over the loss of Tyburn, called the "fury of innovation." The "Mitre" had existed at least from the early part of the seventeeth century, and Johnson was happily spared by death the sight of its approaching abolition in 1788. It would be difficult to exhaust the great subject of Johnson and the "Mitre." His visits were apparently notorious, for within a month after Boswell first met Johnson, Boswell knew that the "Mitre" was Johnson's frequent resort. How Boswell proposed a visit there, and how they supped well, discussed poetry, religion, ghosts, and Boswell's private affairs, and drank two bottles of port, and how they sat till between one and two in the morning—is it not all written in the best biography in the world? Although Johnson dropped the port, and degenerated to water or lemonade, he and Boswell often went again to "keep up the custom of the 'Mitre'"; and, in truth, Johnson had been there before. "Come," said he, "you pretty fools," to the two young women from Staffordshire who consulted him on the subject of Methodism—"Come, you pretty fools, dine with Maxwell and me at the 'Mitre,' and we will talk over that subject:" and they did. But perhaps we had better leave the "Mitre."

We can see Johnson, on some more decorous day, walking along Fleet Street. It must not be in early life, or early morning. In early life Johnson endured "the patron and the jail," and early morning he rarely saw, unless it was very early morning. He found, as we do now, that in London "the day does not go with the sun"; and Johnson, unless obliged by work, or tempted by Burton's "Anatomy of Melancholy," did not rise till noon. It should not be late, for the dark and ill-paved streets are not too safe, and had not Johnson been himself attacked? Let it be after his morning bedroom reception. He dresses in an untidy bushy grey wig, a plain brown suit, black worsted stockings, and shoes with silver buckles—buckles and wigs just survived him.

The sedan chairs and the coaches, the ballad singers, the street cries, the street signs, so serviceable for chairmen and porters who could not read numbers, the men as well as the women wearing coloured clothes, the clergy and physicians in their gowns, all make the streets lively. Even later Charles Lamb could say, " I often shed tears in the motley Strand for fulness of joy at so much life." Johnson rolls through it in that strange way which made people stare. It is daytime, and he does not laugh so as to be heard at the other end of Fleet Street. But he goes along talking to himself, and tapping posts, or mysteriously picking up orange peel. His sight is bad ; but, as Goldsmith's story proves, he sees the heads on the top of Temple Bar. Johnson passes Butchers' Row, where Guy Fawkes had met his fellow-conspirators, and where the Law Courts now stand. He passes Clements Inn and Clifton's eating-house, which he sometimes used ; he passes Essex Street, where, at the " Essex Head," he was to establish his last Club. He may call at a house which was afterwards the first London residence of George Eliot, and was in Johnson's day called the "Turk's Head." It was at the corner of Catherine Street. " I encourage this house," said Johnson, " for the mistress of it is a good, civil woman, and has not much business." He passes Exeter Street, where he first lodged, and lived upon fourpence-halfpenny a day, and the shop of the good bookseller, Wilcockes, of whom he and Garrick had in those early days borrowed a five-pound note; and so to Exeter Change, where, for half a crown, Pidcock showed lions and tigers, whose roars frightened the passing horses. Thence to the "Fountain Tavern," where Johnson read "Irene" to Peter Garrick, and where "Simpson's" now stands. Then came Northumberland House, the northern front of which was twice rebuilt in Johnson's time; and finally Charing Cross. It was then a narrow place without Trafalgar Square, but there, as we all know, he found the "full tide of human existence." If Johnson had turned off before he reached Charing Cross, be sure it was to Garrick's new house in the Adelphi, or to Dr. Burney's, near St. Martin's Lane; or perhaps to visit either Tom's Coffee House, or Wills, or the shop of Davies the bookseller, who had the famous "pretty wife," and who introduced Boswell to Johnson. Or Johnson proceeding, might reach more distant haunts beyond Charing Cross—say the "British Coffee House" in Cockspur Street, or Dodsley's, the bookseller's shop, in Pall Mall, or he would cross Leicester Fields to Reynolds's house; or push further west to St. James's Square, where, in lack of a lodging, he and Savage had, in earlier years, walked round all night and sworn to stand by their country.

ROUND THE TOWN WITH JOHNSON

If Johnson desire to return another way, he has to cross the river or return by boat.

Luckily, old Westminster Bridge, the bridge upon which Wordsworth wrote his famous sonnet, had been opened in 1750. But, if the walk be before 1768, there is no crossing at Blackfriars, where Daniel Deronda was to meet the waiting Mordecai.

The river is pleasant and safe, except in shooting London Bridge. There are at Hungerford, or the Temple Stairs, many small boats rowed by jolly young watermen in red stockings. Johnson is used to this mode of conveyance. He had gone with Boswell more than once on the Thames. But one practice, which time has not spared, but which was at least as old as Addison's "Sir Roger de Coverley," startles us. People passing on the river abuse each other, and are, if possible, satirical. Now, although Mr. Burke afterwards admired it, should we not have been shocked to hear Johnson, the great lexicographer, the stern moralist, reply, as he did from his boat, to some ribaldry, by exclaiming, "Sir, your wife, under pretence of keeping a bawdy-house, is a receiver of stolen goods"! Johnson, on this occasion, may be considered to return by the Temple Stairs, and that early; but this is really most unusual. Sometimes he would dine or drink tea with Mrs. Williams, the head of his odd charitable house; but he seldom came home till two in the morning. Let us hope he had come back earlier on that memorable night when at three in the morning Beauclerk and Langton knocked him up for a "frisk."

We have not time to see Johnson at the houses of his friends or acquaintances or at his clubs. "Round the town," is of course in public places. Now, London at that time had few theatres; but it had many spas and tea gardens, and such places of recreation. Johnson, like a philosopher, defended their existence, and, like a wise man, went to them. "Sir, I am a great friend to public amusements, for they keep people from vice." There are many recorded instances of Johnson's visits to public places. At Marylebone Gardens, when there was an attempt to cheat him and others of the fireworks, I regret to find that he seems to have aided and abetted in a riot. But it was at Vauxhall and Ranelagh that we find the chief public places of an age when responsibility for the universe had not been invented, and man dared to give his soul a loose.

I wish I could show you Johnson at Vauxhall Gardens, for they witnessed the gaiety of seven generations, and were in their prime in Johnson's day. Boswell refers to and praises them. He rightly foresaw a long future for Vauxhall, so "peculiarly adapted to the taste of the English nation." Mr. Austin Dobson has described Vauxhall for us. In Johnson's day Goldsmith and Horace Walpole, Fielding and Smollett, all refer to this place, with walks "so intricate that the most experienced mothers have often lost themselves in looking for their daughters"; and these gardens endured to be again described by Thackeray. Johnson must, of course, have been there. Rowlandson represents him in a picture as supping at Vauxhall. But, alas! there is no record of a visit. As to the other famous place, Ranelagh, he knew it well. Ranelagh was a public garden at Chelsea, opened at a cost of more than £12,000 in 1742, when Johnson was busy giving the "Whig dogs" the worst of it in his parliamentary debates. Ranelagh lasted till twenty years after Johnson's death. It was the predecessor of "Venice in London." The admission was usually one shilling. There were to be found a rotunda and a lake, and a Venetian pavilion, and also trees and alleys, and boxes for refreshments. It was called by Horace Walpole "an immense amphitheatre full of little alehouses." There were public suppers and concerts. It was at first very fashionable, and Lord Chesterfield said he had "ordered all his letters to be directed thither." It must once have been a merry, yet proper place; for the expression "Ranelagh Girl" became common, and, happily, did not mean one who belonged to what has been called the "oldest profession in the world," but a "lively young lady of excellent principles." Long before Johnson died Ranelagh seems to have declined somewhat in public favour. Fireworks and a mimic Etna were introduced, and masquerades and Sunday teas were tried. It was then suggested that the "Fall of Man" should be exhibited in a masquerade. Johnson admired Ranelagh. On his first visit he must have been in low spirits, for he saw in it " only struggles for happiness." But he recovered, and went often, for he deemed it a " place of innocent diversion." Yet he used still to name it amongst the public places in which a barrister must not often be seen. "And, sir, there must be a kind of solemnity in the manner of a professional man."

This imperfect tribute to the glories of Ranelagh brings me almost round the town; for we have journeyed, not, indeed, from "China to Peru," but from Whitechapel to Chelsea. We have not time to see Johnson home, where poor blind Mrs. Williams would sit up for him, and paw the victuals, and, perhaps, put her fingers inside the cups to find whether they were full. It is late, and we must soon leave Johnson. Where may he be safely left? Well, say at the Pantheon in Oxford Street, in the company of two Scotchmen. In truth, we must not pass in silence by the glorious Pantheon, now a wine store, but in Johnson's later years a sort of "winter Ranelagh." Its dignified life was short; for it was only opened in 1772, and it was burnt down within twenty years. But it was deemed a fine building, and was certainly adorned with statues of pagan gods and of George III. That king visited it, and so did Horace Walpole, and Gibbon, and Garrick; and so, on Tuesday, March 31, 1772, did Johnson with Boswell. It was Johnson's first visit. It was long since the other first visit—to

Ranelagh—and Johnson was in better spirits. He had arrived at the years which bring the philosophic mind, and he was "ready now to call a man a good man upon easier terms" than he was formerly. And at the Pantheon did he not talk with a certain Mrs. Bosville from Yorkshire, whom he found a "mighty intelligent lady"? Boswell declared "there was not half a guinea's worth of pleasure in seeing this place." But Johnson replied, "Sir, there is half a guinea's worth of inferiority to other people in not having seen it." Boswell then doubted if there were many happy people there. "Yes, sir," rejoined Johnson, "there are many happy people here. There are many people here who are watching hundreds, and who think hundreds are watching them."

And so Johnson surely showed his wisdom, and would not be cheated, or let others be cheated, of a simple pleasure. In fact, Johnson had one excellent qualification for going round the town, for we are told he "disliked much all speculative desponding considerations." I hardly dare to think what Johnson would have said of the member of a recent Parliament who, speaking of another member, said he would expose his *cui bono* in all its hideous deformity. But it is certain that Johnson hated "a *cui bono* man." "Sir," said he to Boswell, who was demanding reasons, "Sir, it is driving on the system of life." Thus was Johnson, in his genial hour, one of those friends of the human race, the enemies of too much gravity; thus could he keep the balance true between his mortal and his immortal part. Johnson, like the rest of us, had not discovered the final secret of happiness, but his face was set in the right way, and he, like Horace, englished by Johnson's favourite Dryden, had not forgotten that—

> " Happy the man, and happy he alone,
> He who can call to-day his own,
> He who, secure within, can say,
> To-morrow do thy worst ; for I have liv'd to-day.
> Be fair, or foul, or rain, or shine,
> The joys I have possess'd, in spite of fate, are mine.
> Not Heaven itself upon the past has power :
> But what has been, has been, and I have had my hour."

PLAQUE ON JOHNSON'S HOUSE IN GOUGH SQUARE.

DR. JOHNSON AS A TRAVELLER

A Paper read before the Johnson Club

BY

GEORGE WHALE

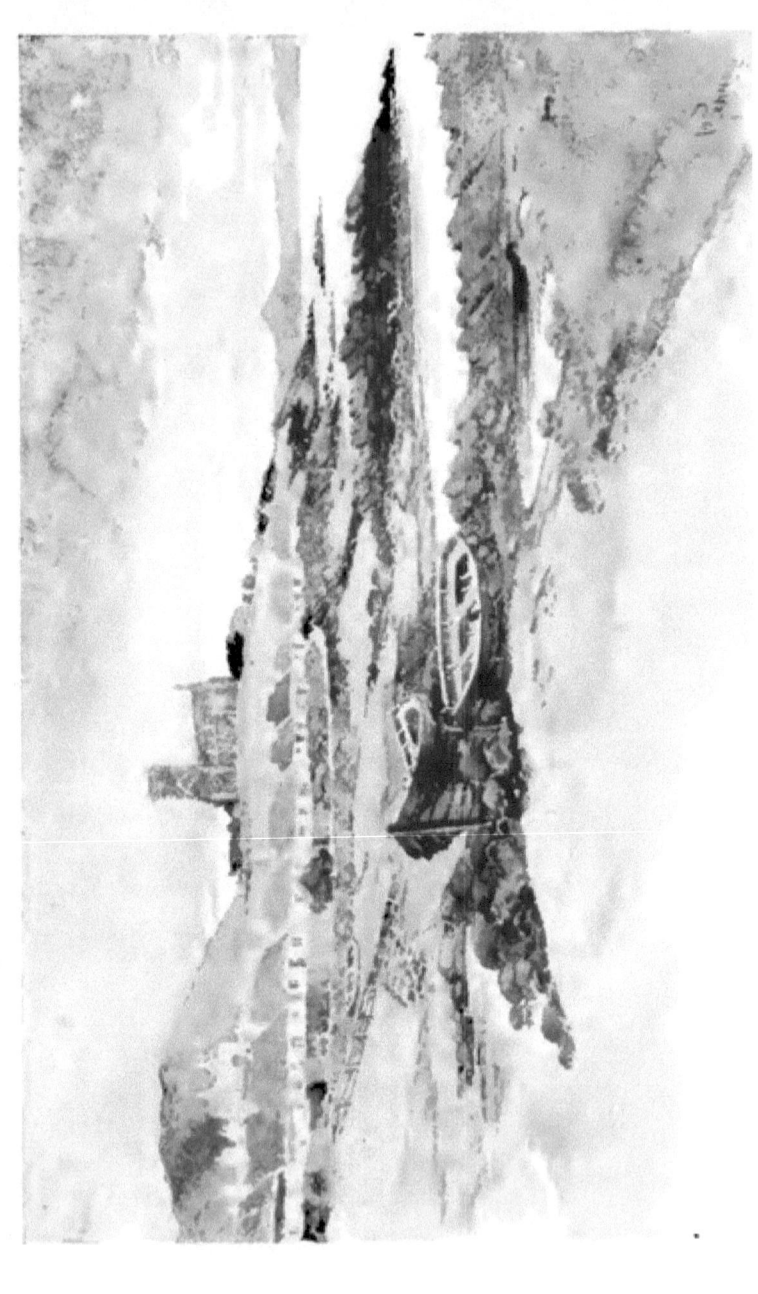

Dr. Johnson as a Traveller

In justifying or in praising the famous man whose name our Club has taken, it is sometimes necessary to attack delusions. Dr. G. B. Hill has shown what a slight basis there is for the popular idea as to Johnson's politics. I propose to show how groundless are the received opinions as to the cockneyism of Johnson.

Every one who knows nothing else of Johnson has heard his sayings showing his fondness for London, and his lack of interest in rural scenery,[1] and many have read some rather misleading remarks on this subject in an essay by Lord Macaulay. Hence it has been too hastily assumed that Johnson was no traveller, and cared nothing for travelling.

Concerning Johnson's sayings on travelling, as on other subjects, it is always necessary to remember that

[1] See "Round the Town with Dr. Johnson," p. 241.

the art of conversation, as he understood it, permitted him to talk for victory, and that although a bishop (Johnson never thought of contradicting a bishop) compared Johnson's talk to an antique statue, Johnson, amongst his friends, admitted that nobody talked more loosely than he did. Hence, his talk was not always consistent. But if we look closely into the matter, we find that Johnson was a writer and a reader of travels; a traveller, too, and a lover of travel. Hence, I am not in the desperate case of the divine who says that if there be nothing to say *about* his text, he speaks round about it. But let us "proceed by steps," as Sir Fitzroy Kelly used to say in the Court of Exchequer, and also when his coachman drove into the ditch.

Johnson had his theory of travel, and if it may be expressed in a word or two, I should say it was this: Do not begin too young; but when prepared, travel much, and enlarge your experience.

Macaulay represents that " of foreign travel Johnson spoke with the force and boisterous contempt of romance." He evidently has in his mind a passage in Boswell,[1] in which Johnson really condemned only the fashionable grand tour, that great institution of the last century for ruining youths of eighteen, when they—

> "Sauntered Europe round
> And gathered every vice on Christian ground."

The poets and the philosophers of the last century

[1] Ed. Hill, iii. p. 352.

had satirised or condemned it, and the so-called "bad" Lord Lyttleton was not the only one who dated his moral ruin from that grand tour, when he "fought two duels, and found the women all Armida's."[1]

Yet Johnson was no enemy to travel, but, in truth, a friend. Many incidental remarks in his writings and conversations render it certain had he read, as we can read, Gibbon's list of precious and indispensable "requisites of foreign travel," Johnson would have agreed with it; for these "requisites" are "age, judgment, a competent knowledge of men and books, and a freedom from domestic prejudices."[2] Johnson, indeed, went himself to the bottom of the matter when, on Good Friday, 1778, he was entertaining Boswell at breakfast, and the talk fell on travel. "A man," said Johnson, "must carry knowledge with him if he would bring home knowledge." Readers of the "Sentimental Journey" will here be reminded of Sterne's exclamation, "I pity the man who can travel from Dan to Beersheba, and cry 'Tis all barren,' and so it is; and so is all the world to him who will not cultivate the fruit it offers."

Johnson would have all travellers cultivate the fruit of travel; and, in addition to many hints in his talk and letters, he has in the *Idler*[3] discoursed on the

---

[1] See "On the Grand Tour," Sir G. O. Trevelyan's "Fox," p. 64; Boswell, iii. p. 458.

[2] Autobiography, p. 269.

[3] 1760, No. 97. "Johnson's Works," iv. pp. 433-5.

proper way to write books of travel. "Few books," he says, "disappoint their readers more. The greater part of travellers tell nothing, because their method of travelling supplies them with nothing to be told. . . . He only is a useful traveller who brings home something by which his country may be benefited." On this principle we find him refusing to publish an account of his travels in France, and advising Boswell not to write of his travels on the continent. These countries were so well known, and the world requires to learn something from books. In fact, for once Johnson says he is anxious that "Corsican Boswell" should not be laughed at. Travellers who did not profit and make others profit by their travels were false to Johnson's theory, and such defection was visited with merited anger and contempt. "Dr. Johnson," says Mrs. Thrale, "was very angry with a gentleman at our house for not being better company, and urged that he had travelled into Bohemia and seen Prague." "Surely," added he, "the man who has seen Prague might tell us something new and something strange, and not sit silent for want of matter to put his lips in motion."

Johnson advised his friends to travel everywhere. "The great object of travelling is," says he, "to see the shores of the Mediterranean." Twice he urged Boswell to go to Spain, and once inspired him with so great an enthusiasm for visiting the Wall of China, that Boswell had gone to see it were it not for his children. This excuse Johnson tried to brush aside, and urged the journey. "Sir," said he, "by doing so you would be doing what would be of importance in raising your children to eminence. There would be a lustre reflected upon them from your spirit and curiosity. They would be at all times regarded as the children of a man who had gone to view the Wall of China." Here Boswell must have smiled, for he adds that Johnson wound up this exhortation by adding, "I am serious, sir."

Johnson's theory of travel embraced China, and, in truth, a survey of mankind "from China to Peru." Johnson, in his "Journey to the Hebrides," records a visit to Mull, and, reflecting on its unkind climate, he concludes that "all travel has its advantages. If the traveller visits better countries he may learn to improve his own; and if fortune carries him to worse he may learn to enjoy it." These are cheerful, if obvious, reflections. Johnson's theory, however, touched more than the surface of things. There was what Wordsworth calls—

> "Some happy tone
> Of meditation slipping in between
> The beauty coming and the beauty gone."

Johnson visits Iona and says, in a passage much admired in his own day, that "whatever withdraws us from the power of our senses, whatever makes the past, the distant, or the future predominate over the present, advances us in the dignity of thinking beings. . . . That man is little to be envied whose patriotism would not gain force upon the plains of Marathon, or whose piety would not grow warmer among the ruins of Iona."

It is not too much to say that if Johnson had a passion for London it sometimes yielded to a conflicting passion for travel. There was no melancholy acquiescence in those pleasures which were, as he deemed them, "only struggles for happiness."

As a lad he read books of travel; and when in poverty at Pembroke College the Master heard him soliloquising thus, "Well, I have a mind to see other places of learning. . . . I'll go to France and Italy." This was but the first of many dreams, for, in imagination at least, Johnson was "always roaming with a hungry heart," and, like the hero of George William Curtis's charming little book, "Prue and I," he fancied himself in many places. Ireland, Holland, the Baltic, Sweden, Poland, and other parts of the continent of Europe were thus in a fashion visited from Fleet Street. So were Cairo and the West Indies. To the day of his death Johnson would fain have seen Italy had his means allowed, and, when sixty-three years old, he thought of going in the king's ship *Endeavour* with Sir Joseph Banks and other men of science about to start on a tour round the world. But travel was a costly luxury then, and the "eternal want of pence" vexed Johnson sore. The college dream was in the brave days when he was twenty-one, and he was sixty-six ere he crossed the Channel for the first and only time in his life.

Meanwhile, however, Johnson had been manfully making the best of it, as to travel as well as many other things. But the best of it was not much. From the time he came to London (1737), aged twenty-eight, till he was about twice twenty-eight, Johnson seems to have left London but rarely. For twenty-five years he never went to Lichfield, his birth-place, and for more than twenty he never saw Oxford. Once he went to Appleby in Leicestershire, but only to try unsuccessfully for a school. When he was in his fiftieth year his mother died, and he was too poor to go to her funeral at Lichfield. Three years more had to elapse before Johnson could for the first time revisit his native place for a few days. No wonder that Johnson had already declared to Bishop Percy that his first twenty years in London had not been very happy.

Yet, if cheerfulness was not "always breaking in," as with Johnson's old college friend Edwards, twice at least in these narrow days Johnson travelled to Oxford and enjoyed himself. In July, 1754, the Dictionary was drawing towards an end, but Johnson said he could not finish it to his mind without visiting the libraries at Oxford, and so to Oxford he went, probably for the first time since he left it in 1729. Thomas Warton says Johnson collected nothing there for his Dictionary. The only certain thing is that he stayed almost five weeks, visited his old college and his old friends, felt himself a more considerable man than most of them, and was treated as such by all, except Dr. Radcliffe, then Master of Pembroke. Again, four years later, Johnson visited Oxford, proudly wore the gown which the honorary M.A. gave him, and permitted University College to witness him drink three bottles of port without being the worse for it. Very probably it was on the same day, and possibly in his gown, that Johnson challenged Dr. Vansittart to climb over a wall.

But these were rare holidays. It is clear that poverty generally chained up Johnson in London, till, in 1762, he first had his pension.[1] Then his passion for travel broke forth immediately. The first quarterly allowance was paid to Johnson about the 20th July, 1762, and on the 16th August he and Sir Joshua, then Mr. Reynolds, were off on a jaunt of about seven weeks in Devonshire—Reynolds's native county. There they fared sumptuously every day; Johnson gave his soul a loose, and Reynolds for the only time in his life saw Johnson drunk. On most occasions— even in a whole night of festivity—Johnson trusted himself with nothing stronger than tea and lemonade.[2] Yet never did he willingly abstain from holiday making. The Devonshire excursion was the first of

[1] See Appendix B, vol. iii. Boswell's Johnson. Ed. Hill.
[2] See " Round the Town with Dr. Johnson," p. 247.

many. In November of the same year, having applied for his October allowance (somewhat in arrear), he was off again to Oxford, and thenceforth every year of his life saw him quit London. There are many recorded visits to Oxford and to Lichfield and to Ashburn (where lived the Rev. Dr. Taylor, the schoolfellow and Whig friend of Johnson). Others were make in Kent, Surrey, Essex, Devon, Northamptonshire, Wales ; and some more to Birmingham, Cambridge, and Brighton. There was a visit to France ; and, above all, there was the famous tour of nearly four months in Scotland.

In his travels Johnson sometimes walked from one midland town to another ; and as he used to say that when they came to London, he only had $2\frac{1}{2}$d. in his pocket, and Garrick $1\frac{1}{2}$d., it is probable that Garrick's declaration "we rode and tied," was but a boast. Johnson, however, was physically incapable of being a good walker. It was one thing to roll along Fleet Street, and quite another, as he found, to walk in the Isle of Rasay. So Boswell had to explore alone. Many of Johnson's journeys were done by coach. He and Boswell would take the "post-coach" to Oxford, and Frank, the servant, " came in the heavy coach." But this was slow work. It took twenty-six hours to go to Lichfield. The roads were bad, and "for many years after the middle of the century stage coaches had no springs."[1] Hence Johnson, in his pension days, went

[1] Lecky, "History of England," vi. p. 179, and Boswell, i. p. 340 n.

in a post-chaise. Thus he rode to Scotland, and thus he travelled with the Thrales, and thus he loved to travel. "In the afternoon," says Boswell, "as we were driven rapidly along in the post-chaise, he said to me, 'Life has not many things better than this.'" In the post-chaise the moralist struggled with the traveller. Whilst being driven towards Derby Johnson said, "If I had no duties, and no reference to futurity, I would spend my life in driving briskly in a post-chaise, with a pretty woman; but" (and this too is very characteristic) "she should be one who could understand me, and would add something to the conversation."[1]

To relate what was seen on most of Johnson's tours were impossible. Boswell and others, fortunately, give the conversations; and they are, to us, worth much more than mere itineraries. Of the French tour only a few short particulars are given by Boswell, and of the Welsh tour in 1774 a brief diary, unknown to Boswell, was secretly preserved by Johnson's servant, Francis Barber, and published in 1816. Of the Scotch journey, however, in 1773, all the world knows there is Johnson's own narrative (1775) and Boswell's Journal (1785). It has been said that Johnson appears greater in Boswell's books than in his own; and it is certain that more has been learnt from Boswell's Journal than from Johnson's rather solemn work. That does not reveal to us the

[1] Cf. Prior, Poem *The Secretary*.

DR. JOHNSON AS A TRAVELLER

"Great Cham of literature," as Boswell has enabled us to see him. Who can forget that "full suit of plain brown clothes, with twisted hair buttons of the same colour, a large bushy greyish wig, a plain shirt, black worsted stockings, and silver buckles," the English oak stick and the brown great coat, with pockets large enough to hold the folio Dictionary. That stick is particularly memorable in connection with Johnson's travels. Boswell more than once mentions it, and relates how it served as a support and as a measure. Alas, it was lost in Mull, what time Johnson, riding on a little horse that could scarcely support his weight, entrusted the precious stick to a Scot, whom even Boswell calls a "fellow." That stick they saw no more. "Ho, ho, my friend," said Johnson, "it is not to be expected that any man in Mull who has got it will part with it. Consider, sir, the value of such a piece of timber here."

"This will be a great treasure to us some years hence," said Johnson to Boswell, as, during the tour, he looked over Boswell's Journal. A treasure it has proved. Although it records that Johnson called a mountain a "considerable protuberance," it also gives us many of the good things said and done during a journey called by Boswell the "Transit of Johnson over the Caledonian Hemisphere," and by Boswell's father, the old Whig judge, "Going over Scotland with a brute."[1] It is clear that in Scotland, if there

[1] See Rowlandson's set of caricatures of this journey.

were sometimes plain living (once it was but bread and lemon) there was also high thinking; and sometimes high words. Not to speak of that apocryphal debate with Adam Smith, there was the awful and inevitable combat which arose between Johnson and Lord Auchinleck, when in a collection of medals one was found bearing the image of Oliver Cromwell.

The general impression we get from the records of Johnson's travels is that whether in Scotland or in Oxford, or elsewhere, he was very much the Johnson of London: loving books, but, as Madame D'Arblay says, preferring a man of the world to a scholar. The "note" of Johnson as a traveller was, if about him I may use a Scotch phrase, "wake-mindedness." Johnson suffered from a certain insensibility to natural, or rather rural, beauty. This was the fault of the age rather than the man. A yellow primrose was but a yellow primrose for the true eighteenth century Englishman. It is more worthy of notice that Johnson, in all his travels, showed that strong mental curiosity, that invincible desire to die learning, which is the true dividing line between the intelligent and dull. Still more important is it to remember that Johnson had his full share, and more than his full share, of the best spirit of his age, and that, as a traveller, he never forgot that, abroad as well as at home, human life is the great object of interest.

AT THE "CHESHIRE CHEESE"

BY

LIONEL JOHNSON

THE EMBLEMS OF THE CLUB.
(Drawn by Joseph Pennell, Brother of the Johnson Club.)

At the "Cheshire Cheese"

WITH the best of goodwill, but rough numbers, I raise
To our excellent selves a song-offering of praise:
Away with mock modesty! We are the men
Who love to live now as the *Doctor* lived then.
For his writings . . . 'tis true that not all of us read
    them:
But we walk in his ways, and his precepts, we heed
    them;
The *town* and its taverns, the sound of the street,
To the genuine *Johnsonian* are merry and sweet.
"The country is sweeter," you say, sir? Why, no,
    sir:
A dull misanthropical prig may think so, sir!
Let him babble alone of green fields at a distance:
For us, *Charing Cross's* "full tide of existence!"
But the place of our pride we love best to remember
Is the *Cheshire Cheese, Fleet Street, Thirteenth of
    December:*

When the *Brethren*, all eager and bright, flock together,
Johnsonianissimi, birds of a feather:
When the *Scribe* gives the word for beginning the revel,
And everything dismal is sent to the devil:
When the *Chaplain* has murmured his brief *Benedicite*,
And we sit on "the thrones of all human felicity"
(Which is how, you must know, "tavern chairs were defined
By the *Great Lexicographer's* accurate mind):
When nobody bothers us, critic or creditor,
Client, constituent, contributor, editor;
When we're done for awhile with all worry and work,
Free and easy as any unspeakable *Turk*:
When for winter's worst weather we care not a jot,
But the fogs and the winds and the rains are forgot
In the pipe-bowl so ruddy, the punch-bowl so hot:
When the firelight goes dancing around the old wall,
And glows on our glasses and us, one and all,
And our feast is the bravest for miles round *Saint Paul*!
Then the wits pour the wine of their wit at its best,
And the rafters are ringing with infinite zest:
While the *Prior* makes it plain to the meanest capacity
That he champions the chair with uncommon tenacity,

AT THE "CHESHIRE CHEESE"

Standing no nonsense, nor any audacity.
Oh! then is the height of our pleasure and pride,
As we sit in good fellowship trusty and tried.
If the *Doctor* himself were to join our festivity
Would the *Brethren* submit to his tongue with passivity?
(For if the dear *Doctor* were sharing our punch,
And daring that perilous pudding to munch,
He might call us "you dogs," and say "he'd have a frisk with us,"
But he'd "down" us as well, and be mightily brisk with us.)
Certain *Brethren*, may be, would meet more than their match,
And some would soon talk of the trains they must catch;
Having caught quite enough from the tongue of the *Sage*,
Whose ways have not probably altered with age;
For, as Browning has sung, he was "ever a fighter,"
And I'm sure he fights still, at some heavenly *Mitre*.
But *Brethren* there are who would fight to the last,
And be fresh as at first, when the "good talk" was past:
They would soothe the huge Talker, smooth him, disarm him,
Fortiter face him and *suaviter* charm him;
(Though sundry *Whig* principles well might alarm him):

And perhaps, if the *Great Man were* tamed, and all *was* well,
He'd give us his honest opinion of *Boswell*.
If only it might be ! . . . But, long as we may,
We shall ne'er hear that laughter, *Gargantuan* and gay,
Go pealing down *Fleet Street* and rolling away.
In silence we drink to the silent, who rests
In the warmth of the love of his true lovers' breasts.

UNWIN BROTHERS, THE GRESHAM PRESS, WOKING AND LONDON.

www.ingramcontent.com/pod-product-compliance
Lightning Source LLC
Chambersburg PA
CBHW030809230426
43667CB00008B/1126